Help Me! Guide to the Samsung Galaxy S 5

By Charles Hughes

D1569621

Table of Contents

Getting Started 8

   1. Button Layout 8

   2. Charging the Galaxy S5 13

   3. Turning the Galaxy S5 On and Off / Restarting the Phone 14

   4. Navigating the Screens 15

   5. Types of Home Screen Objects 16

   6. Organizing Home Screen Objects 17

   7. Transferring Files to the Galaxy S5
      Using a PC or Mac / Inserting a microSD Card 25

Making Calls 28

   1. Dialing a Number 28

   2. Calling a Contact 30

   3. Calling a Frequently Dialed Number 32

   4. Returning a Recent Phone Call 35

   5. Receiving a Voice Call... 37

   6. Using the Speakerphone during a Voice Call 39

   7. Using the Keypad during a Voice Call 41

   8. Using the Mute Function during a Voice Call........... 42

   9. Switching to a Bluetooth Headset during a Voice Call.............. 42

   10. Starting a Conference Call (Adding a Call)................. 44

   11. Redialing the Last Dialed Number........................... 44

Managing Contacts.. 45

   1. Adding a New Contact.. 45

   2. Finding a Contact 47

3. Editing Contact Information.. 48

4. Deleting a Contact 50

5. Assigning a Photo to a Contact... 52

6. Sharing a Contact's Information.. 56

7. Backing Up Contacts... 61

8. Adding a Contact to a Group 61

9. Adding a Contact to Favorites 63

10. Adding a Contact to the Reject List 63

11. Adding a Contact Shortcut to the Home Screen 65

12. Joining or Separating Contact Information of Two Contacts 65

Text Messaging 67

1. Composing a New Text Message 67

2. Copying, Cutting, and Pasting Text 70

3. Using the Auto-Complete Feature 72

4. Switching to another Language 73

5. Receiving Text Messages 73

6. Reading Text Messages 75

7. Forwarding Text Messages... 76

8. Calling the Sender from within a Text................................ 77

9. Viewing Sender Information from within a Text.................... 78

10. Deleting Text Messages 79

11. Adding Texted Phone Numbers to Contacts..................... 80

12. Adding an Attachment to a Text Message......................... 84

13. Attaching a Picture 86

14. Attaching a Video 90

15. Attaching a Voice Recording 91

16. Attaching a Memo.. 93

17. Attaching a Calendar Event 95

18. Saving Attachments from Text Messages 97

19. Sending a Text Message to an Entire Group..................... 99

20. Managing Favorite Text Message Recipients.................... 101

Taking Pictures and Capturing Videos **105**

    1. Taking a Picture 105

    2. Using the Digital Zoom 106

    3. Using Both Cameras at Once 107

    4. Using the Flash 110

    5. Applying an Effect before Taking a Picture 111

    6. Setting the Camera Mode 113

    7. Creating an Animated Photo 114

    8. Creating a Panoramic Photo 116

    9. Capturing a Video 117

    10. Taking a Picture while Capturing a Video 118

    11. Setting the Camcorder Mode 118

    12. Editing Camera and Camcorder Settings 120

Managing Photo and Video Albums **122**

    1. Browsing Photos and Videos 122

    2. Starting a Slideshow 125

    3. Editing a Photo 128

    4. Tagging a Person in a Photo 138

    5. Trimming a Video 140

    6. Deleting Photos and Videos 141

    7. Moving Photos between Albums 142

    8. Creating a Photo Collage 144

Using the Chrome Web Browser **147**

    1. Navigating to a Web Page 147

    2. Adding and Viewing Bookmarks 148

    3. Managing Browser Tabs 151

    4. Working with Links 153

    5. Searching a Web Page for a Word or Phrase 154

    6. Viewing the Browsing History 156

    7. Sharing a Web Page 157

    8. Setting the Search Engine 158

    9. Turning Autofill On or Off 160

10. Saving Passwords 162

11. Turning Pop-Up Blocking On or Off 164

12. Changing the Text Size 166

13. Clearing Personal Data 168

Using the Email Application 171

1. Adding an Email Account to the Phone 171

2. Reading Email (Email App) 174

3. Sending an Email (Email App) 175

4. Replying to and Forwarding Emails (Email App) 177

5. Deleting Emails and Restoring
   Deleted Emails to the Inbox (Email App) 179

6. Searching the Inbox (Email App) 181

7. Blocking All Emails from a Specific Sender 182

Using the Gmail Application 184

1. Adding a Google Account to the Phone 184

2. Reading Email (Gmail App) 189

3. Sending an Email (Gmail App) 190

4. Replying to and Forwarding Emails (Gmail App) 192

5. Deleting Emails and Restoring
   Deleted Emails to the Inbox (Gmail App) 194

6. Adding Labels to Emails 198

7. Searching the Inbox (Gmail App) 200

8. Ignoring New Messages in a Conversation 201

9. Blocking All Emails from a Specific Sender 201

10. Adjusting the General Gmail Preferences 202

11. Adjusting Gmail Account Preferences 206

Managing Applications 208

1. Setting Up a Google Account 208

2. Searching for an Application 209

3. Buying an Application 214

4. Uninstalling an Application 216

5. Adding an Application to Your Wishlist 218

6. Hiding Applications on the Application Screen 220
7. Closing Applications Running in the Background 222
8. Organizing Application Icons into Folders 223
9. Installing a Previously Purchased Application 226
10. Updating Installed Applications 227
11. Switching between Google Accounts 227

Using the S Voice Assistant 229

1. Calling, Sending Messages, and Taking Notes 229
2. Searching the Web for General Information 230
3. Finding Information about Music and Movies 230
4. Navigating to a Webpage 230
5. Finding Locations and Attractions 231
6. Looking Up Times and Dates 231
7. Asking about the Weather 232

Adjusting the Wireless Settings 233

1. Setting Up Wi-Fi 233
2. Setting Up Bluetooth 237
3. Turning Airplane Mode On or Off 239
4. Enabling or Disabling the Mobile Network 241
5. Turning Data Roaming On or Off 243
6. Turning Near Field Communication On or Off 244

Adjusting the Sound Settings 246

1. Setting the Vibration Intensity 246
2. Setting the Ringtone, Media, and Alarm Volume 250
3. Setting the Default Ringtone 252
4. Setting the Default Vibration Pattern 253
5. Setting the Default Notification Sound 255
6. Turning Ringer Vibration On or Off 256
7. Turning System Sounds On or Off 257

Adjusting the Display Settings 258

1. **Adjusting the Brightness** 258
2. **Changing the Wallpaper** 261
3. **Turning Multi Window On or Off** 264
4. **Turning Auto-Rotate On or Off** 265
5. **Setting the Screen Timeout** 267
6. **Changing the Font** 268
7. **Setting the Touch Key Light Duration** 271
8. **Turning the Battery Percentage On or Off** 273
9. **Turning High Touch Sensitivity On or Off** 276
10. **Setting the Home Screen Mode** 276
11. **Turning Motions and Gestures On or Off** 277
12. **Turning Air View On or Off** 280
13. **Customizing the LED Notification Light** 282

Adjusting the Security Settings 284

1. **Setting Up Screen Lock Protection** 284
2. **Changing the Automatic Lock Time** 289
3. **Making Passwords Visible** 291
4. **Allowing the Installation of
   Applications from Unknown Sources** 293

Adjusting the Language and Input Settings 294

1. **Changing the Phone Language** 294
2. **Adding an Input Language** 299
3. **Personalizing Text Prediction** 302
4. **Turning Swype On or Off** 304

Tips and Tricks 305

1. **Maximizing Battery Life** 305
2. **Adding an Extension to a Contact's Number** 306
3. **Checking the Amount of Available Memory** 306
4. **Calling a Number from a Website** 306
5. **Locking Text Messages** 307
6. **Entering Alternative Characters** 307

7. Using MP3's as Ringtones 307
8. Capturing a Screenshot without
   Connecting the Phone to a Computer 308
9. Viewing All Quick Settings Icons in the Notification Bar 308
10. Clearing a Single Notification 308
11. Blocking Calls, Notifications, Alarms, and the LED Indicator 308
12. Viewing a Video while Using Another Application 309
13. Making the Phone Open
    Applications and Menus Faster (Advanced Tip) 309
14. Making the Home Button More Responsive 310
15. Hiding Personal Files 311

Troubleshooting 312

1. Galaxy S5 does not turn on 312
2. Galaxy S5 is not responding 313
3. Can't make a call 313
4. Can't surf the web 314
5. Screen or keyboard does not rotate 314
6. Low microphone volume, caller can't hear you 314
7. Display does not adjust brightness automatically 314
8. Application does not install correctly 315
9. Touchscreen does not respond as expected 315
10. Phone becomes very hot 315
11. Camera does not turn on 315

Index 316

Getting Started

Table of Contents

1. Button Layout
2. Charging the Galaxy S5
3. Turning the Galaxy S5 On and Off / Restarting the Phone
4. Navigating the Screens
5. Types of Home Screen Objects
6. Organizing Home Screen Objects
7. Transferring Files to the Galaxy S5 Using a PC or Mac / Inserting a microSD Card

1. Button Layout

The Galaxy S5 has three hard buttons, two soft keys, a microUSB 3.0 port, and a headphone jack, which perform the following functions:

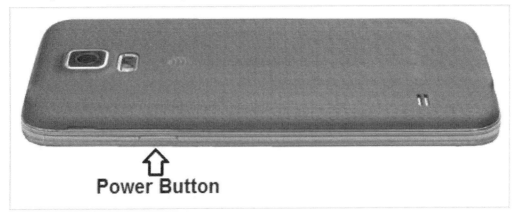

Figure 1: Right Side View

Power Button - Turns the phone on and off. Locks and unlocks the phone.

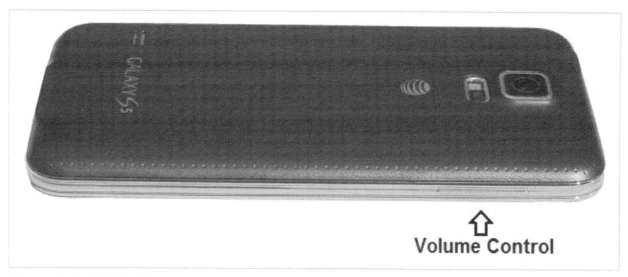

Figure 2: Left Side View

Volume Control - Controls the volume of the ear piece, speaker phone, and music.
The soft keys only appear when the screen is turned on. Touch each button to perform the
corresponding action:

Figure 3: Front View

Back Key - Returns the phone to the previous screen or menu.

Recent Apps Key - Opens a list of open applications. Refer to *"Managing Applications"* on page 208 to learn more about apps on the S5. This key also acts as a Menu key when you press and hold it.

Home Button (not a soft key) - Returns the phone to the Home screen.

Fingerprint Scanner - Allows you to scan your fingerprint to register it and to unlock the phone. Refer to *"Setting Up Screen Lock Protection"* on page 284 to learn more about unlocking the S5 using your fingerprint.

Note: The menu key that used to exist to the left of the Home button on the Galaxy S 4 has been replaced by the Recent Apps key. Press and hold the Recent Apps key to make it act like the retired Menu key.

microUSB 3.0 Port

Figure 4: Bottom View

microUSB 3.0 Port (accessed by opening the bottom cover) - Connects the phone to a computer in order to transfer data. Although the port is significantly different from previous generations, you may still use your old charger (from the S4 or another Android phone) to charge the S5. However, using a USB 3.0 cable (included with the S5) will allow you to transfer files to and from your computer much faster.

Figure 5: Top View

Headphone Jack - Allows headphones or an AUX cable to be plugged in to the phone.

2. Charging the Galaxy S5

In order to prolong the battery life, try discharging (below 20%) and recharging the phone to 100% at least once a month. While the phone is charging, "Charging" appears on the Lock screen below the date, as shown in **Figure 6**. When the phone is fully charged, "Charged" appears on the Lock screen below the date. Refer to *"Turning the Battery Percentage On or Off"* on page 273 to learn how to turn the exact battery percentage on or off.

Figure 6: Charging Screen

3. Turning the Galaxy S5 On and Off / Restarting the Phone

To turn the Galaxy S5 on, press and hold the **Power** button for three seconds. "Samsung Galaxy S5" appears and the phone starts up.

To turn the phone off, press and hold the **Power** button until the Device Options menu appears, as shown in **Figure 7**. Touch **Power off**. A confirmation dialog appears. Touch **OK**. The Galaxy S5 shuts down. You can also touch **Restart** in the Device Options menu to restart the Galaxy S5.

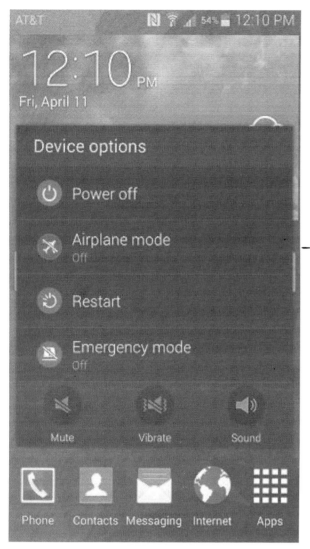

Figure 7: Device Options Menu

4. Navigating the Screens

There are many ways to navigate the screens of the Galaxy S5. Use the following tips:

- Press the **Home** button to return to the Home screen at any time. The last viewed Home screen will appear. Press the **Home** button again to view the main Home screen. Any application that is currently in use will be in the same state when it is re-opened.
- Slide your finger to the left or right to access additional Home screens from your main Home screen.
- Touch the ⬑ key at any time to return to the previous screen, menu, or application. Once you are at the main Home screen, the ⬑ button has no function.\

- Touch the top of the screen and move your finger down to view all notifications.

5. Types of Home Screen Objects

Each Home screen on the Galaxy S5 is fully customizable. Refer to *"Organizing Home Screen Objects"* on page 17 to learn how to customize the Home screens. Each screen can hold one or more of the following items:

- **Widget** - A tool that can be used directly from the Home screen without having to open it first like an application. Widgets usually take up the whole screen or a fraction of it, while applications are added as icons. The Calendar widget is shown in **Figure 8**. Touching one of the days on the calendar allows you to view the events that occur on that day, and create and edit new events.
- **Application** - A program that opens in a new window, such as a game. Applications are added to the Home screen as icons.
- **Folder** - A folder containing application icons. Please note that a folder cannot store widgets. Refer to *"Organizing Application Icons into Folders"* on page 223 to learn more.

Figure 8: Calendar Widget

6. Organizing Home Screen Objects

Customize a Home screen by adding, deleting, or moving around application icons and widgets. The Galaxy S5 allows you to customize seven Home screens. Refer to *"Types of Home Screen Objects"* on page 16 to learn more about them.

To add an application icon to a Home screen:

1. Touch the ▦ icon in the lower right-hand corner of the Home screen. The Apps screen appears, as shown in **Figure 9**.

2. Touch the screen and move your finger to the left or right to browse the applications and widgets that are installed on your phone. The applications and widgets appear.
3. Touch and hold an application icon. The Home screen appears, as shown in **Figure 10**. Do not release the screen yet.
4. Drag the icon to the desired location. If there is no room on the current screen, drag the icon to the left or right edge of the screen, or on top of a Home screen thumbnail. The adjacent Home screen appears.
5. Release the screen. The application icon is placed on the selected Home screen.

To add a widget to a Home screen:

1. Touch and hold the key. The Home Screen Editing menu appears, as shown in **Figure 11**.
2. Touch **Widgets** at the bottom of the screen. A list of widgets appears, as shown in **Figure 12**.
3. Touch and hold a widget in the list, such as 'Calendar'. The Home screen appears. Do not release the screen yet.
4. Drag the widget to the desired location. If there is no room on the current screen, drag the icon to the left or right edge of the screen, or on top of a Home screen thumbnail. The adjacent Home screen appears.
5. Release the screen. The widget is placed on the selected home screen, as shown in **Figure 13** with the Calendar widget.

To delete an application icon or widget from a Home screen:

1. Touch and hold an application icon or widget. The phone briefly vibrates and "Remove" appears at the top of the screen, as shown in **Figure 14**. Do not release the screen.
2. Drag the icon over 'Remove'. The icon turns red.
3. Release the screen. The application icon or widget is deleted from the Home screen.

Note: To move an object to another location on the Home screen, touch and hold the object until the phone briefly vibrates and "Remove" appears at the top of the screen. Move the object to the desired location and release the screen. The object is placed in the new location. You cannot place an object on a page that is full or on top of another object, unless it is a folder.

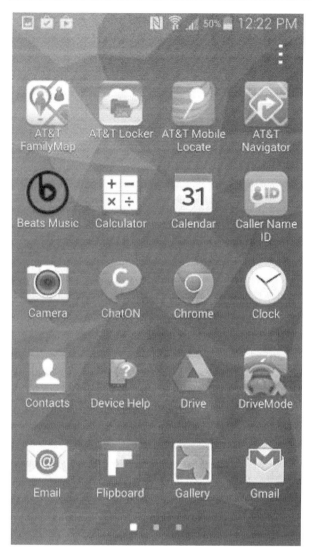

Figure 9: Application Screen

Figure 10: Home Screen (while adding, moving, or deleting application icons)

Figure 11: Home Screen Editing Menu

Figure 12: List of Widgets

Figure 13: Calendar Widget

Figure 14: Deleting an Application Icon or Widget

7. Transferring Files to the Galaxy S5 Using a PC or Mac / Inserting a microSD Card

Media files that you have obtained elsewhere can be imported to the Galaxy S5. To import media:

1. Connect the Galaxy S5 to your PC or Mac using the provided USB cable. "Connected as a media device" appears in the status bar. The PC automatically recognizes the Galaxy S5, but the Mac needs an additional application in order to transfer files to the phone. If you are using a Mac, download the Android File Transfer application at **www.android.com/filetransfer/** before proceeding.
2. Open **My Computer** (or **Computer** on Windows Vista or later) on a PC and double-click the 'Galaxy S5' portable device. On a Mac, open the Android File Transfer program. The Galaxy S5 folder opens.
3. Double-click the **Phone** folder or **Card** folder (if using a microSD card), if you are using a PC. The Galaxy S5 Folders appear on a PC, as shown in **Figure 15**, or on a Mac, as shown in **Figure 16**.
4. Double-click a folder. The folder opens.
5. Drag and drop a file into the open folder. The file is copied and will appear in the corresponding library.

The 'Card' folder only appears (step 3 above) if you have a microSD card inserted into the phone. To insert a microSD card:

1. Carefully remove the back cover by wedging a fingernail in the provided tab to the left of the camera and pulling back on the cover. The plastic seems fragile, but it is actually quite strong.
2. Remove the battery. You do not necessarily need to turn off the phone, but make sure that you save anything that might be lost when the phone is turned off.
3. Insert the microSD card (up to 128GB), as shown in **Figure 17**.
4. Replace the battery and the back cover. You may now turn on the phone.

Note: When copying eBooks to the Galaxy S5, drag and drop the files into the corresponding folder. For instance, eBooks you wish to read using the Kindle Reader for Android should be copied to the 'kindle' folder.

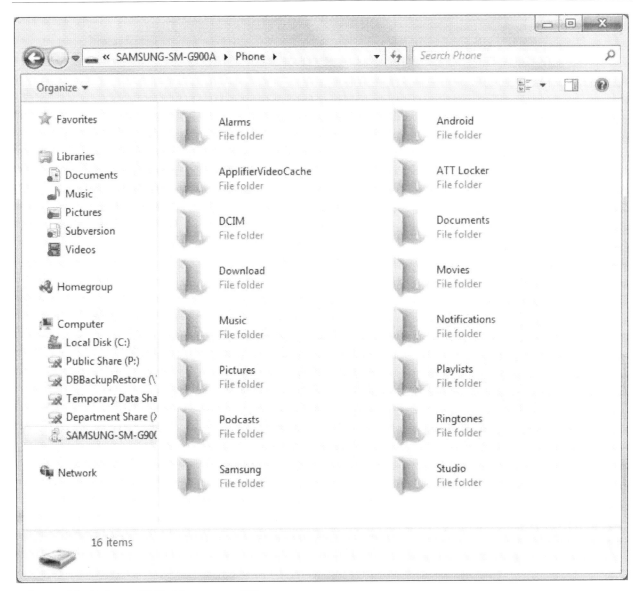

Figure 15: Galaxy S5 Folders on a PC

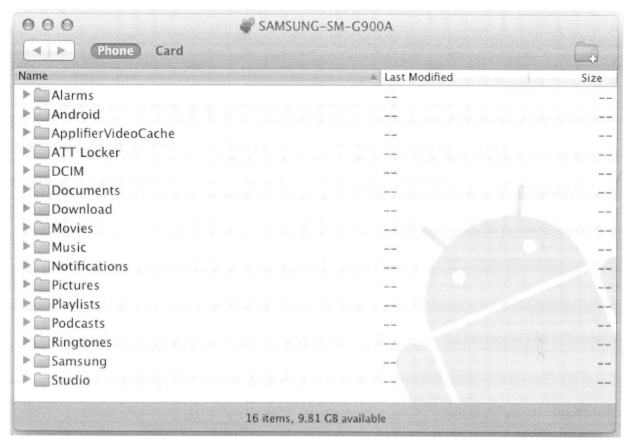

Figure 16: Galaxy S5 Folders on a Mac

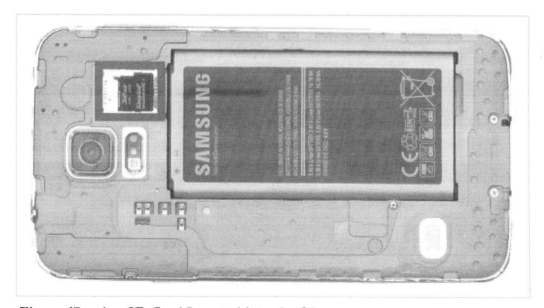

Figure 17: microSD Card Inserted into the S5

Making Calls

Table of Contents

1. Dialing a Number
2. Calling a Contact
3. Calling a Frequently Dialed Number
4. Returning a Recent Phone Call
5. Receiving a Voice Call
6. Using the Speakerphone During a Voice Call
7. Using the Keypad During a Voice Call
8. Using the Mute Function During a Voice Call
9. Switching to a Bluetooth Headset During a Voice Call
10. Starting a Conference Call (Adding a Call)
11. Redialing the Last Dialed Number

1. Dialing a Number

Numbers that are not in your phonebook can be dialed on the keypad. To manually dial a phone number, touch the 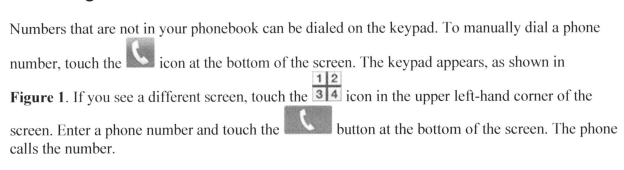 icon at the bottom of the screen. The keypad appears, as shown in **Figure 1**. If you see a different screen, touch the icon in the upper left-hand corner of the screen. Enter a phone number and touch the button at the bottom of the screen. The phone calls the number.

Figure 1: Phone Keypad

2. Calling a Contact

If a number is stored in your Phonebook, you may touch the name of a contact to dial it. Refer to *"Adding a New Contact"* on page 45 to learn how to add a contact to the Phonebook. To call a contact already stored in your Phonebook:

1. Touch the 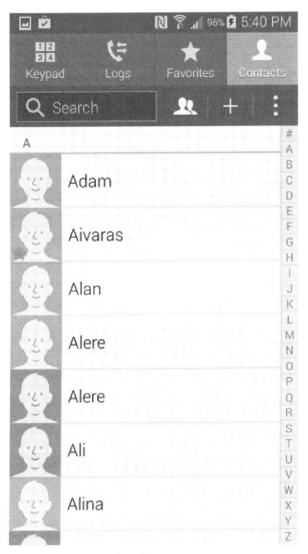 icon at the bottom of the Home screen. The Phonebook appears, as shown in **Figure 2**.
2. Touch a contact's name. The Contact Information screen appears, as shown in **Figure 3**.
3. Touch the number that you wish to call. The S5 dials the number.

Figure 2: Phonebook

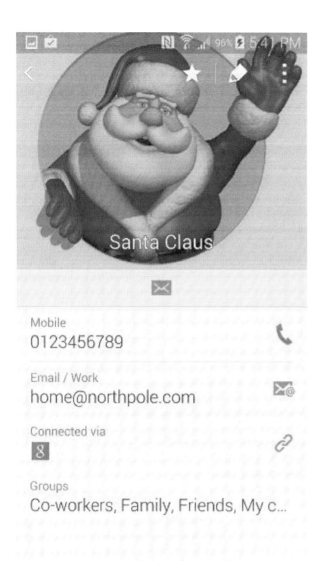

Figure 3: Contact Information Screen

3. Calling a Frequently Dialed Number

You can add a Direct Dial shortcut to the Home screen, which immediately dials a number stored in your phonebook when you touch the shortcut. To add and use a Direct Dial shortcut:

1. Touch and hold the key. The Home screen editing menu appears, as shown in **Figure 4**.
2. Touch **Widgets** at the bottom of the screen. A list of widgets appears, as shown in **Figure 5**.
3. Touch the screen and move your finger to the left. Additional widgets appear.
4. Touch the widget. A list of Contact Widget options appears.
5. Touch and hold the **Direct Dial** widget. The main Home screen and a group of thumbnails representing the other Home screens appear, as shown in **Figure 6**. Do not release the screen yet.
6. Drag the icon to the desired location and release the screen. If you wish to place the Direct Dial icon on an alternate home screen, hold the icon over one of the Home Screen thumbnails shown in **Figure 6**. The icon is placed and the Phonebook appears.
7. Touch the name of a contact. The Direct Dial shortcut is set and appears on the Home screen, provided that there is only one number assigned to the contact. Otherwise, a list of phone numbers appears. Touch a phone number in the list to assign it to the Direct Dial.
8. Touch the **Direct Dial** icon. The number is dialed.

Figure 4: Home Screen Editing Menu

Figure 5: List of Widgets

Figure 6: Home Screen while Adding the Direct Dial Icon

4. Returning a Recent Phone Call

After you miss a call, the Galaxy S5 will notify you of who called and at what time. The phone also shows a history of all recent calls. To view and return a missed call or redial a recently entered number:

1. Touch the ![icon] icon at the bottom of the screen. The keypad appears.

2. Touch the ![icon] icon at the top of the screen. A list of recent calls appears, as shown in **Figure 7**.

3. Touch the name of a contact and slide your finger to the right. The phone calls the selected contact.

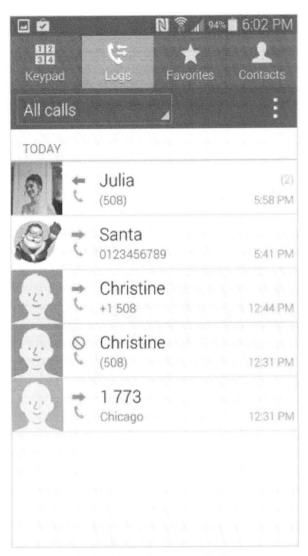

Figure 7: Full List of Recent Calls

5. Receiving a Voice Call

When receiving a voice call, the Incoming Call screen appears, as shown in **Figure 8**. To answer

the call, touch the ![call icon] icon and drag it to the right side of the screen. The call is connected. To

decline the call, touch the ![decline icon] icon and drag it to the left side of the screen. The call is sent to
voicemail.

If you are in the middle of using an application, a pop-up appears, as shown in **Figure 9**.

Touch **Answer** to answer the call, or touch **Reject** to reject it. You may also touch the ![speaker icon] icon
to answer the call and immediately turn on the speakerphone.

Figure 8: Incoming Call Screen

Figure 9: Incoming Call Pop-Up

6. Using the Speakerphone during a Voice Call

The Galaxy S5 has a built-in Speakerphone, which is useful when calling from a car or when several people need to participate in a conversation. To use the Speakerphone during a phone call:

1. Place a phone call. The Calling Screen appears, as shown in **Figure 10**.

2. Touch the ![Speaker icon] icon at the bottom of the screen. The speakerphone turns on.

3. Adjust the volume of the Speakerphone using the Volume Controls. Refer to *"Button Layout"* on page 8 to locate the Volume Controls.

4. Touch the icon. The speakerphone turns off.

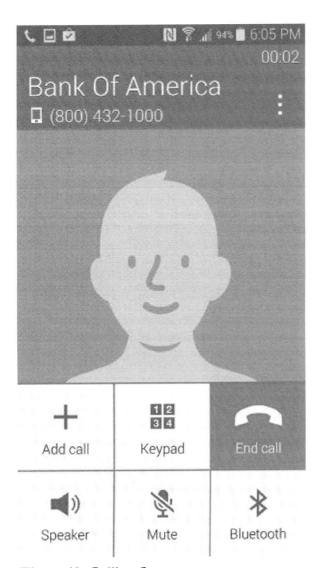

Figure 10: Calling Screen

7. Using the Keypad during a Voice Call

You may wish to use the keypad while on a call in order to input numbers in an automated menu or to enter an account number. To use the keypad during a voice call, place the call and touch

the 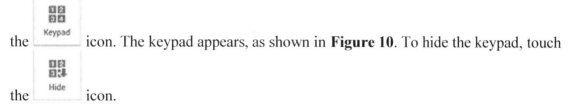 icon. The keypad appears, as shown in **Figure 10**. To hide the keypad, touch

the icon.

Figure 11: Phone Keypad While on a Call

8. Using the Mute Function during a Voice Call

During a voice call, you may wish to mute your side of the conversation. When mute is turned on, the person on the other end of the line will not hear anything on your side. To use Mute during a

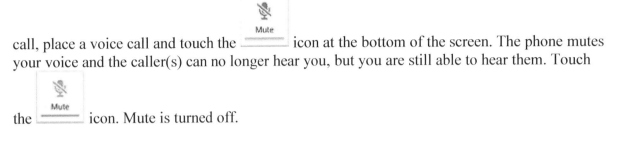

call, place a voice call and touch the ⎯⎯⎯ icon at the bottom of the screen. The phone mutes your voice and the caller(s) can no longer hear you, but you are still able to hear them. Touch

the ⎯⎯⎯ icon. Mute is turned off.

9. Switching to a Bluetooth Headset during a Voice Call

While on a call, you can switch to your paired Bluetooth headset at any time, if one is connected. Refer to *"Setting Up Bluetooth"* on page 237 to learn how to set up your headset. Touch

the Bluetooth icon. If the headset is already connected, you can now use it on the voice call. If the headset is not connected, the Select Device screen appears, as shown in **Figure 11**. Touch

the Bluetooth icon to disconnect from the headset.

Figure 12: Select Device Screen

10. Starting a Conference Call (Adding a Call)

To talk to more than one person at a time, place a new call without ending the current one. To add a call:

1. Place a call. The call is connected and the Calling screen appears.

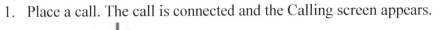

2. Touch the Add call icon at the bottom of the screen. The keypad appears.

3. Dial a number and touch the [button icon] button at the bottom of the screen, or touch the [contact icon] icon at the top of the screen and touch a number in your phonebook. The phone dials the second number.

4. Touch [Merge icon] once connected. The calls are merged and a three-person conference call is started.

11. Redialing the Last Dialed Number

You may redial the number that you last dialed by touching the [button icon] button at the bottom of the screen. The last dialed number appears above the keypad. Touch the [button icon] button again. The number is redialed.

Managing Contacts

Table of Contents

1. Adding a New Contact
2. Finding a Contact
3. Editing Contact Information
4. Deleting a Contact
5. Assigning a Photo to a Contact
6. Sharing a Contact's Information
7. Backing Up Contacts
8. Adding a Contact to a Group
9. Adding a Contact to Favorites
10. Adding a Contact to the Reject List
11. Adding a Contact Shortcut to the Home Screen
12. Joining or Separating the Contact Information of Two Contacts

1. Adding a New Contact

The Galaxy S5 can store phone numbers, email addresses, and other contact information in its Phonebook. To add a new contact to the Phonebook:

1. Touch the ![icon] icon at the bottom of the screen. The Phonebook appears, as shown in **Figure 1**.

2. Touch the ![icon] icon near the top of the screen. The New Contact screen appears, as shown in **Figure 2**.

3. Touch **Device** at the top of the screen to select where the contact will be saved.

4. Touch **Google** to save the contact to your Google account. Alternatively, touch **Device** or **SIM** to save the contact's information to the corresponding location.

5. Touch each field to edit it. Enter the contact's information in each field. You can also touch the ⊕ or ⊖ to add or remove a field, respectively.

6. Touch **Save** in the upper right-hand corner of the screen when you are finished. The contact's information is stored in the Phonebook.

Note: To hide the keyboard at any moment, touch the ⬑ *key. Refer to* "Tips and Tricks" *on page 305 to learn more about adding a new contact, including a tip on adding an extension to a phone number.*

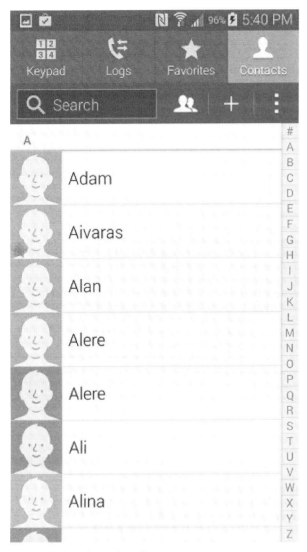

Figure 1: Phonebook

Figure 2: New Contact Screen

2. Finding a Contact

After adding a contact to your phonebook, you may search for it. To find a stored contact:

1. Touch the ![icon] icon at the bottom of the Home screen. The Phonebook appears.
2. Touch **Search** at the top of the screen. The keyboard appears.
3. Start typing the name of the contact that you wish to find. The Galaxy S5 searches as you type, and the possible contact matches appear, as shown in **Figure 3**.

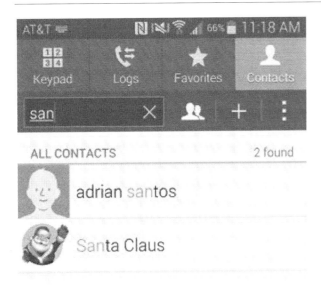

Figure 3: Possible Contact Matches

3. Editing Contact Information

After adding contacts to the Phonebook, you may edit them at any time. To edit an existing contact's information:

1. Touch the ![icon] icon. The Phonebook appears.
2. Touch the name of the contact that you wish to edit. The Contact Information screen appears, as shown in **Figure 4**.
3. Touch the ![icon] icon in the upper right-hand corner of the screen. The Contact Editing screen appears, as shown in **Figure 5**.

4. Touch a field to edit it. Enter the contact's information into each field.
5. Touch **Save** at the top of the screen. The contact's information is updated.

Note: To hide the keyboard at any time, touch the 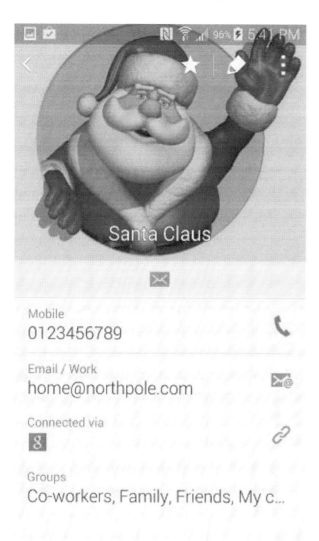 *key.*

Figure 4: Contact Information Screen

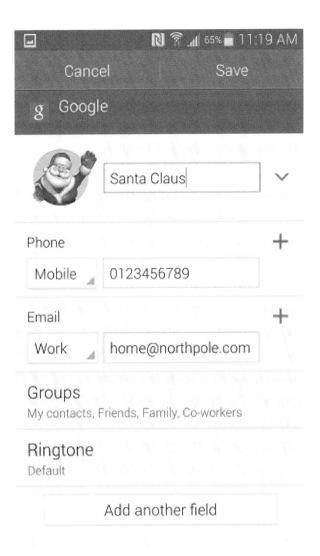

Figure 5: Contact Editing Screen

4. Deleting a Contact

You may delete a contact's information from the Phonebook in order to free up space, or for organizational purposes. To delete unwanted contact information:

1. Touch the ![icon] icon. The Phonebook appears.
2. Touch and hold the name of the contact that you wish to delete. The contact is selected, and a ✔ appears to the left of the contact's name, as shown in **Figure 6**. Touch the names of any additional contacts that you also wish to delete.

3. Touch the 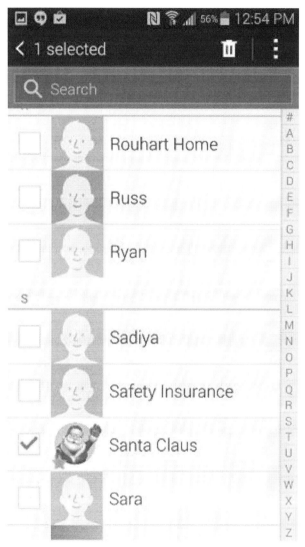 icon in the upper right-hand corner of the screen. A confirmation dialog appears.
4. Touch **OK**. The contact's information is deleted.

Figure 6: Contact Selected

5. Assigning a Photo to a Contact

You can assign a personal photo to a contact, which will appear next to the contact's name in the phonebook, and when the contact calls. An existing photo can be assigned from the Gallery or a picture may be taken and assigned.

To assign a photo from the Gallery to a contact:

1. Touch the 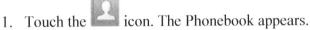 icon. The Phonebook appears.
2. Touch the contact's name. The Contact Information screen appears.
3. Touch the ⬛ icon in the upper right-hand corner of the screen. The Contact Editing screen appears.
4. Touch the ⬛ icon next to the contact's name. The Contact Photo menu appears, as shown in **Figure 7**.
5. Touch **Image**. The Gallery opens, as shown in **Figure 8**.
6. Touch an album. The album opens.
7. Touch a photo thumbnail. The Crop screen appears, as shown in **Figure 9**.
8. Touch the ⬜ icons and drag them in any direction to resize the crop. Touch the center of the photo and drag your finger to select the desired section of the photo. Touch **Done** in the upper right-hand corner of the screen. The photo is assigned to the contact.

To take a picture and assign it to a contact:

1. Follow steps 1-4 above. The Assign Photo menu appears.
2. Touch **Take picture**. The camera turns on. Touch the ⬛ icon if you wish to switch between the front and rear cameras.
3. Touch the ⬛ button at the bottom of the screen. The camera takes a picture and a preview of it appears.
4. Touch **Save** to use the picture or touch **Discard** to retake it. If you touch 'Save', the Crop screen appears.
5. Touch the ⬜ icons and drag them in any direction to resize the crop. Touch the center of the photo and drag your finger to select the correct section of the photo. Touch **Done** in the upper right-hand corner of the screen. The photo that you captured is assigned to the contact.

*Note: Touch the contact's photo, and then touch **Remove** to remove the assigned photo.*

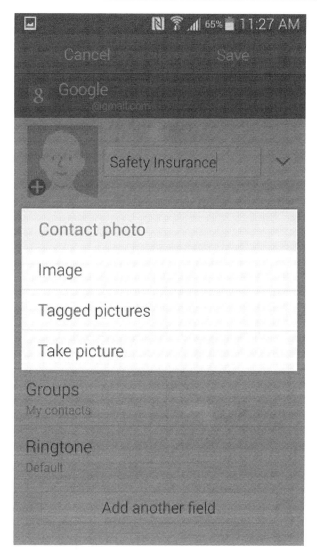

Figure 7: Contact Photo Menu

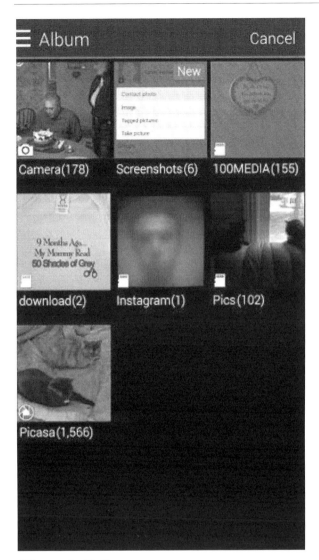

Figure 8: Gallery

Figure 9: Crop Screen

6. Sharing a Contact's Information

When a contact is stored in the phonebook, all of the information for that contact can be shared. To share a contact's information:

1. Touch the ![icon] icon. The phonebook appears.

2. Touch and hold the name of the contact that you wish to share. The ![icon] icon appears in the upper-right hand corner of the screen.

3. Touch the ![icon] icon. The Contact menu appears, as shown in **Figure 10**.
4. Touch **Share namecard**. The Sharing Method menu appears, as shown in **Figure 11**.
5. Touch **Gmail**. The New Email screen appears with the contact's information attached, as shown in **Figure 12**. You can also touch **Messaging**, in which case the New Message screen appears with the contact's information attached, as shown in **Figure 13**.
6. Enter the recipient's email address (or phone number, if sending via text message). The email address is entered.
7. Touch the **Subject** and **Compose** fields to enter a topic for the email, and a message, respectively.
8. Touch the ![icon] button in the upper right-hand corner of the screen, if sending via email.

   Touch the ![icon] button, if sending via text message. The contact's information is sent to the selected recipient.

Note: Sending contact information via Bluetooth is possible but is only for advanced users, and is not discussed in this basic guide.

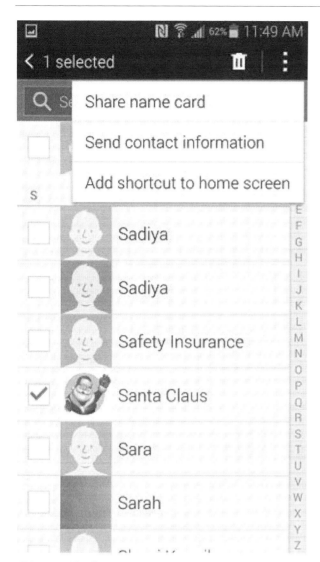

Figure 10: Contact Menu

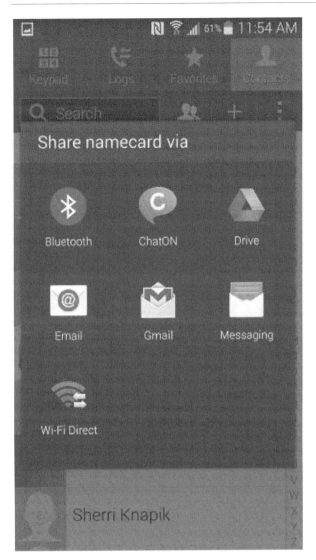

Figure 11: Sharing Method Menu

Figure 12: New Email Screen

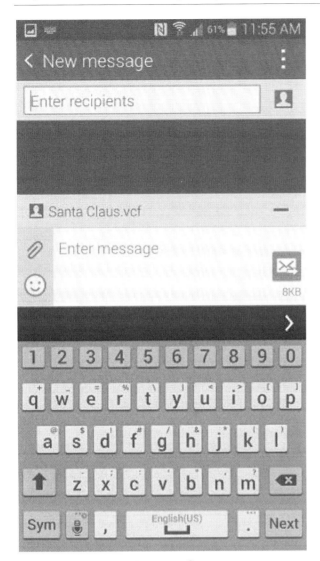

Figure 13: New Message Screen

7. Backing Up Contacts

There is no need to manually back up contacts on your Galaxy S5. When you log in to a Google account, the contacts are automatically backed up on Google's servers and made accessible from any device registered under the same account. If you do not have a Google account, please register at **https://accounts.google.com/signup**.

8. Adding a Contact to a Group

It can be useful to create contact groups, such as 'Family' or 'Co-workers', in order to quickly send text messages or emails to multiple people. To add a contact to a group:

1. Touch the ![icon] icon. The Phonebook appears.
2. Touch the name of the contact that you wish to edit. The Contact Information screen appears.
3. Touch the ![icon] icon in the upper right-hand corner of the screen. The Contact Editing screen appears.
4. Touch **Groups**. A list of groups appears, as shown in **Figure 14**.
5. Touch as many group names as you wish. A ![checkmark] mark appears next to each selected group. You can also touch **Create** at the top of the screen to create a new group.
6. Touch **Save** in the upper right-hand corner of the screen. The contact is added to the selected groups.

Note: You may quickly view your groups by touching the ![icon] *icon at the top of the phonebook.*

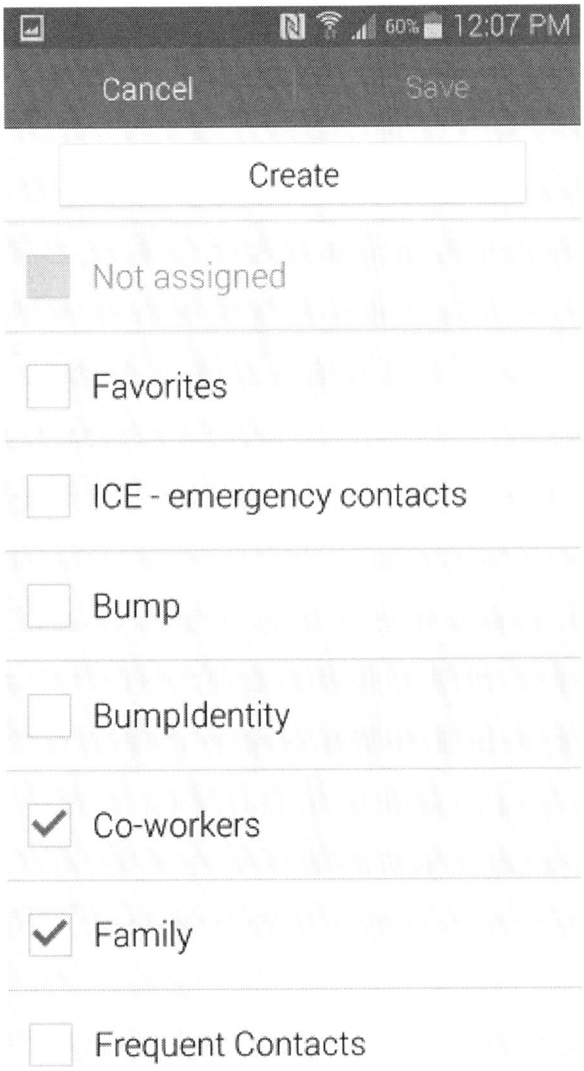

Figure 14: List of Groups

9. Adding a Contact to Favorites

In order to find your most frequently used contacts more quickly, you may wish to add them to your Favorites. To add a contact to Favorites:

1. Touch the ![icon] icon. The Phonebook appears.
2. Touch the contact's name. The Contact Information screen appears.

3. Touch the ![star icon] icon at the top of the screen. The contact is added to your Favorites. To view your favorite contacts, touch **Favorites** at the top of the screen while viewing the keypad, phonebook, or call logs.

10. Adding a Contact to the Reject List

You may wish to block incoming calls from certain unwelcome callers. To add a contact to the Reject list:

1. Touch the ![icon] icon. The Phonebook appears.
2. Touch the contact's name. The Contact Information screen appears.

3. Touch the ![icon] icon in the upper right-hand corner of the screen. The Contact Editing menu appears, as shown in **Figure 15**.
4. Touch **Add to reject list**. Calls received from the selected contact will now be automatically rejected.

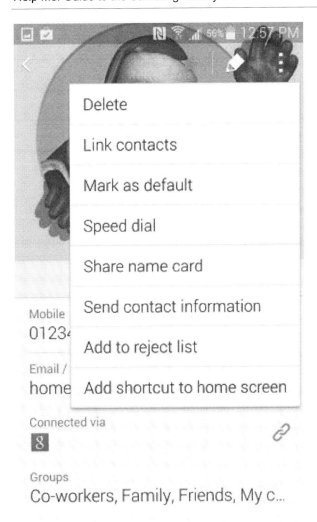

Figure 15: Contact Editing Menu

11. Adding a Contact Shortcut to the Home Screen

In order to call, text, or email a person that you frequently contact, you may wish to add a contact shortcut to the Home screen. To add a contact shortcut:

1. Touch the [icon] icon. The Phonebook appears.
2. Touch the contact's name. The Contact Information screen appears.

3. Touch the [icon] icon in the upper right-hand corner of the screen. The Contact Editing menu appears.
4. Touch **Add shortcut to home screen**. A shortcut to the contact's information is added to the Home screen.

12. Joining or Separating Contact Information of Two Contacts

Sometimes, you may accidentally add contact information for the same person in two separate entries in the Phonebook. Instead of re-entering the information into a single entry, you may join the contacts. To join contact information:

1. Touch the [icon] icon. The Phonebook appears.
2. Touch the name of a contact. The Contact Information screen appears.

3. Touch the [icon] icon in the upper right-hand corner of the screen. The Contact Editing menu appears.
4. Touch **Link contacts**. The Phonebook appears.
5. Touch one or more contacts that you wish to join with the one you selected in step 2.

   A [icon] mark appears next to each selected contact.
6. Touch **Done** in the upper right-hand corner of the screen. The contacts are joined and their joint information will appear under the entry of the one that you selected in step 2.

To separate contact information:

1. Touch the [icon] icon. The Phonebook appears.
2. Touch the name of the contact. The Contact Information screen appears.

3. Touch the ▣ icon in the upper right-hand corner of the screen. The Contact Editing menu appears.
4. Touch **Unlink contacts**. The Linked Contact screen appears, as shown in **Figure 16**.
5. Touch the ⊖ icon next to the contact that you wish to unlink from the entry. A confirmation dialog appears.
6. Touch **OK**. The selected contact is separated from the contact information that you are viewing.

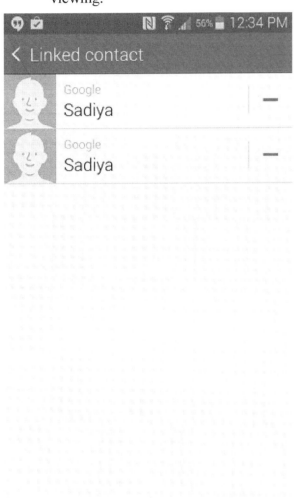

Figure 16: Linked Contact Screen

Text Messaging

Table of Contents

1. Composing a New Text Message
2. Copying, Cutting, and Pasting Text
3. Using the Auto-Complete Feature
4. Switching to another Language
5. Receiving Text Messages
6. Reading Text Messages
7. Forwarding Text Messages
8. Calling the Sender from within a Text
9. Viewing Sender Information from within a Text
10. Deleting Text Messages
11. Adding Texted Phone Numbers to Contacts
12. Adding an Attachment to a Text Message
13. Attaching a Picture
14. Attaching a Video
15. Attaching a Voice Recording
16. Attaching a Memo
17. Attaching a Calendar Event
18. Saving Attachments from Text Messages
19. Sending a Text Message to an Entire Group
20. Managing Favorite Text Message Recipients

1. Composing a New Text Message

The Galaxy S5 can send text messages to other mobile phones. To compose a new text message:

1. Touch the ▧ icon at the bottom of the Home screen. The Messaging screen appears, as shown in **Figure 1**.
2. Touch the ✎ icon in the upper right-hand corner of the screen. The New Message screen appears, as shown in **Figure 2**.
3. Enter the name of a contact or enter a phone number. Suggestions appear while typing. The addressee or phone number is entered.

4. Touch **Enter message** and enter a message. Touch the 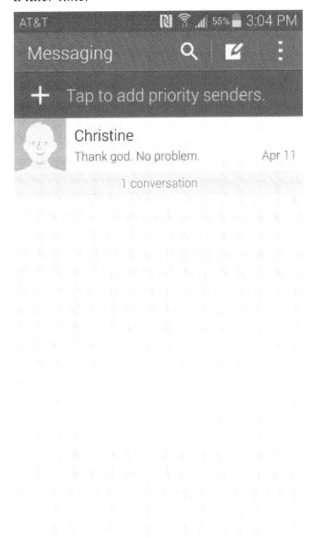 button. The message is sent and appears as a conversation, sorted by send date, as shown in **Figure 3**.

Note: Refer to "Tips and Tricks" *on page 305 to learn how to schedule a text message to be sent at a later time.*

Figure 1: Messaging Screen

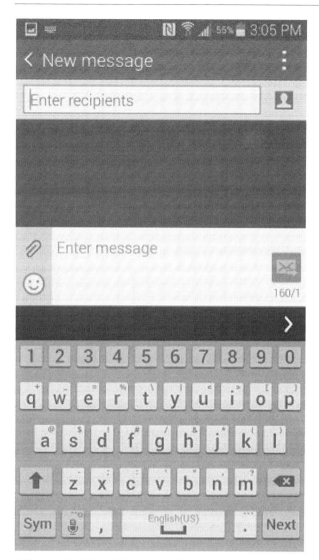

Figure 2: New Message Screen

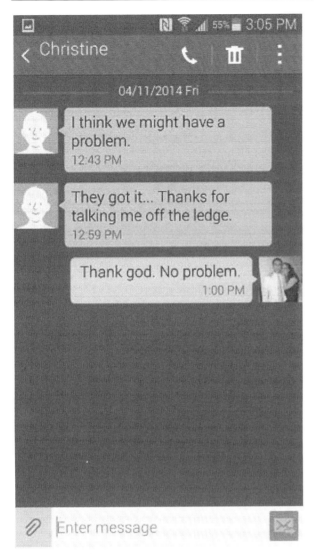

Figure 3: Text Conversation

2. Copying, Cutting, and Pasting Text

The Galaxy S5 allows you to copy or cut text from one location and paste it to another. Copying leaves the text in its current location and allows you to paste it elsewhere. Cutting deletes the text from its current location and allows you to paste it elsewhere. To cut, copy, and paste text:

1. Touch and hold text on the screen. The Text options appear, as outlined in **Figure 4**. To learn how to compose a message, refer to *"Composing a New Text Message"* on page 67.
2. Touch one of the following options to perform the associated action:

- **Select All** - Selects all of the text in the field.
- **Cut** - Removes the text while copying it to the clipboard. Touch and hold any white field, even in an outside application, and touch **Paste** to enter the cut text.
- **Copy** - Leaves the text in the field while copying it to the clipboard. Touch and hold any white field, even in an outside application, and touch **Paste** to enter the copied text.

Note: The 'cut' and 'copy' options only become available when text is selected.

Figure 4: Text Options

3. Using the Auto-Complete Feature

While typing a text message, the Galaxy S5 automatically makes suggestions to auto-complete words, which appear above the virtual keyboard, as outlined in **Figure 5**. This is especially useful when a word is very long. To accept a suggestion, touch the word. The word is inserted into the current message.

Figure 5: Auto Suggestions

4. Switching to another Language

While entering a text message, you can switch your keyboard to display a non-English keyboard. Before switching to another keyboard, you must add it via the Keyboard Settings screen. Refer to *"Adding an Input Language"* on page 299 to learn how. To switch to another language, touch the spacebar and slide your finger to the left or right. The alternate keyboard appears.

5. Receiving Text Messages

The phone can receive text messages from any other mobile phone, including non-smartphones. When receiving a text, the phone vibrates once, plays a sound, or both, depending on the settings. Refer to *"Setting the Default Notification Sound"* on page 255 to learn how to set text message notifications.

If the screen is locked, the text message alert appears on the screen, as shown in **Figure 6**. Touch the text message and release the screen. Touch the center of the screen and slide your finger in any direction to unlock the phone and immediately open the text message.

To open a newly received text message when the screen is unlocked, touch the status bar at the top of the screen and drag it down (the bar where the time, battery, and signal bars are located). The Notifications screen appears, as shown in **Figure 7**. Touch the message with the ✉ icon next to it. The new text message opens.

Figure 6: Text Message on the Lock Screen

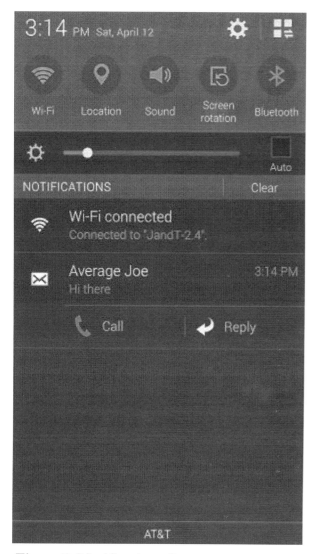

Figure 7: Notifications Screen

6. Reading Text Messages

You may read any text messages that you have received, provided that you have not deleted them.

To read stored text messages, touch the [icon]. The Messaging screen appears. Touch a conversation. The conversation opens.

7. Forwarding Text Messages

The forwarding feature on the phone allows a text message to be copied in full and sent to other recipients. To forward a text message:

1. Touch the icon. The Messaging screen appears.
2. Touch a conversation. The Conversation opens.
3. Touch and hold a text message. The Message options appear, as shown in **Figure 8**.
4. Touch **Forward**. The New Message screen appears with the original message pasted in the message field.
5. Enter a phone number or the name of a contact. The recipient is selected.
6. Touch the button. The text message is forwarded.

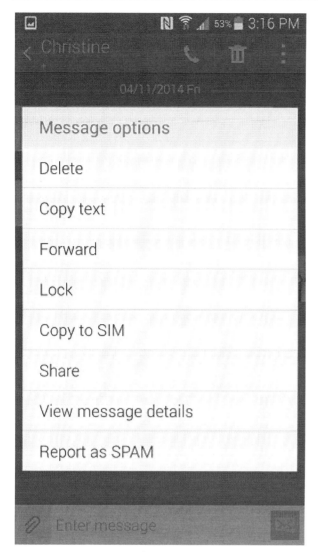

Figure 8: Message Options

8. Calling the Sender from within a Text

After receiving a text message from a contact, you may call that person without exiting the text message. To call someone while viewing a text conversation, put the phone up to your ear. The Galaxy S5 automatically dials the contact's number.

9. Viewing Sender Information from within a Text

You can look up a contact's details without exiting the Messaging application. To view the information of the person who sent you a text message, open the text conversation. Refer

to *"Reading Text Messages"* on page 75 to learn how. Touch the 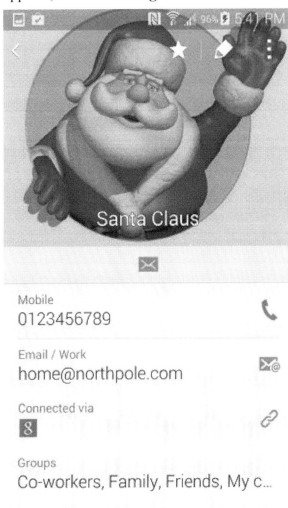 icon or the person's picture next to any one of the messages the he or she has sent. The Contact Information screen appears, as shown in **Figure 9**.

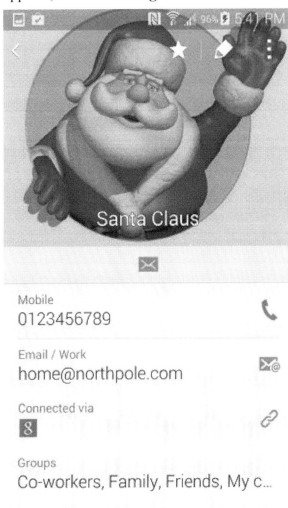

Figure 9: Contact Information Screen

10. Deleting Text Messages

The Galaxy S5 can delete separate text messages or an entire conversation, which is a series of text messages between you and one or more contacts.

Warning: Once deleted, text messages cannot be restored.

To delete an entire conversation:

1. Touch the ⬜ icon. The Messaging screen appears.
2. Touch and hold a conversation. The Conversation is selected and a ✓ mark appears next to it, as shown in **Figure 10**. Touch any additional conversations that you would like to delete.
3. Touch the 🗑 icon in the upper right-hand corner of the screen. A Confirmation dialog appears.
4. Touch **OK**. The conversation is deleted.

To delete a separate text message:

1. Touch the ⬜ icon. The Messaging screen appears.
2. Touch a conversation. The conversation opens.
3. Touch and hold a text message. The Message options appear.
4. Touch **Delete**. A confirmation dialog appears.
5. Touch **OK**. The message is deleted.

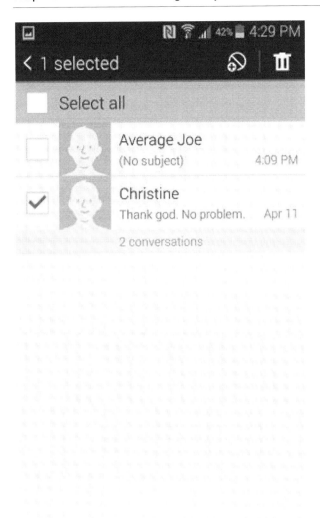

Figure 10: Selected Conversation

11. Adding Texted Phone Numbers to Contacts

A phone number contained in a text message may be immediately added to the phonebook as a new contact. To save a texted phone number as a contact:

1. Touch the ⬜ icon. The Messaging screen appears.
2. Touch a conversation. The conversation opens.
3. Touch the phone number in the text message. The Phone Number options appear, as shown in **Figure 11**.
4. Touch **Add to Contacts**. The Create Contact window appears, as shown in **Figure 12**.

5. Touch **Create contact**, in which case the New Contact screen appears, as shown in **Figure 13**. Refer to *"Adding a New Contact"* on page 45 to learn how to add the number to your Phonebook. Alternatively, touch **Update existing**, in which case the Phonebook appears, as shown in **Figure 14**. Touch the name of an existing contact, and then touch **Save** to add the number to the existing contact's information.

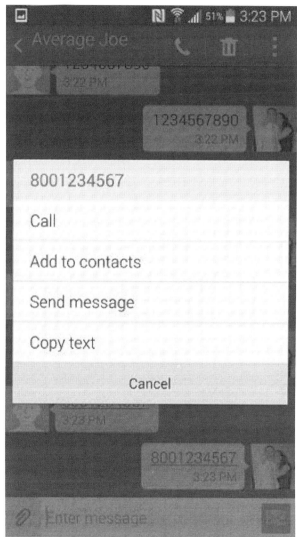

Figure 11: Phone Number Options

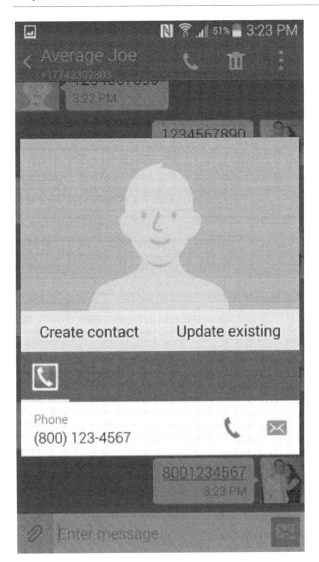

Figure 12: Create Contact Window

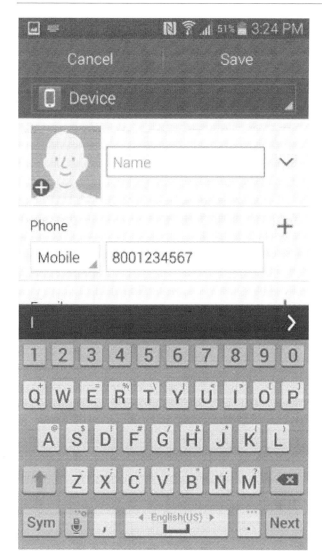

Figure 13: New Contact Screen

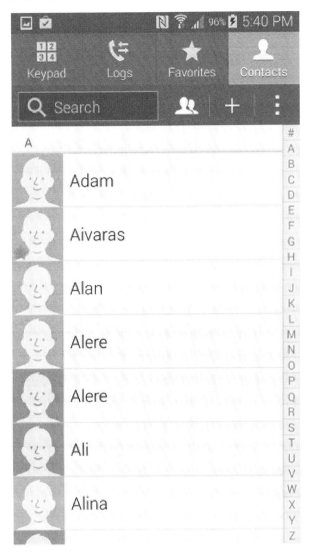

Figure 14: Phonebook

12. Adding an Attachment to a Text Message

A picture, video, or other file can be attached to any text message. To send a text message with an attachment:

1. Refer to *"Composing a New Text Message"* on page 67 and follow steps 1-3.
2. Touch the [paperclip] icon to the left of the 'Enter message' field. The Attachment menu appears, as shown in **Figure 15**.
3. Refer to one of the following sections to learn how to attach the associated media:

- **Attaching a Picture**
- **Attaching a Video**
- **Attaching a Voice Recording**
- **Attaching a Memo**
- **Attaching a Calendar Event**

4. Touch and hold an attachment and then touch one of the following options to manage it, if desired:

   - **View** - Preview the attachment in full-screen mode. Touch the ![key] key to return to the text message.
   - **Replace** - Replace the attachment with another one.
   - **Remove** - Remove the attached file from the text message.

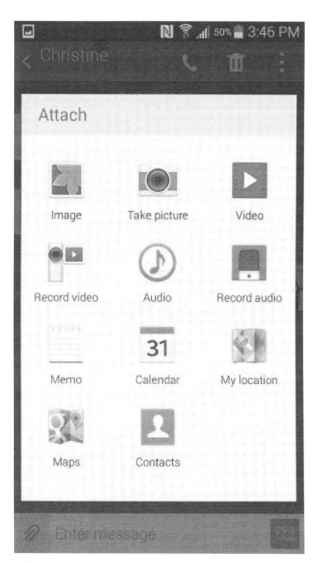

Figure 15: Attachment Menu

13. Attaching a Picture

The Galaxy S5 can send media messages containing pictures. To attach a picture to a text message:

1. Refer to *"Adding an Attachment to a Text Message"* on page 84 and follow steps 1-3. The Attachment menu appears.
2. Follow the steps in the appropriate section below:

Taking and Attaching a Picture

1. Touch the [icon] icon. The camera turns on.
2. Touch the [button] button. The picture is captured and displayed on the screen for review, as shown in **Figure 16**.
3. Touch **Discard** to retake the photo or touch **Save** to attach it to the text message. The photo is attached and the text message appears, as shown in **Figure 17**.

Attaching a Picture from a Photo Album

1. Touch the [icon] icon. The Gallery opens, as shown in **Figure 18**.
2. Touch the album that contains the photo that you wish to attach. The thumbnails of the photos in the album appear.
3. Touch a photo. A [checkmark] mark appears on the selected photo.
4. Touch **Done** in the upper right-hand corner of the screen. The photo is attached and the text message appears.

Figure 16: Picture Review

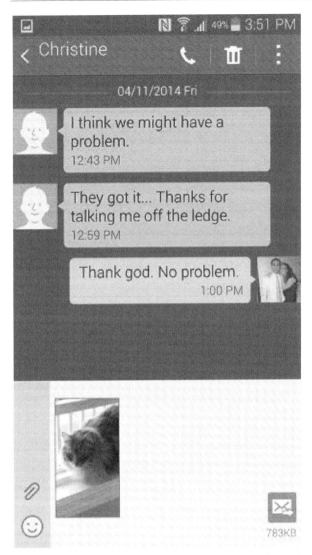

Figure 17: Text Message with Picture Attached

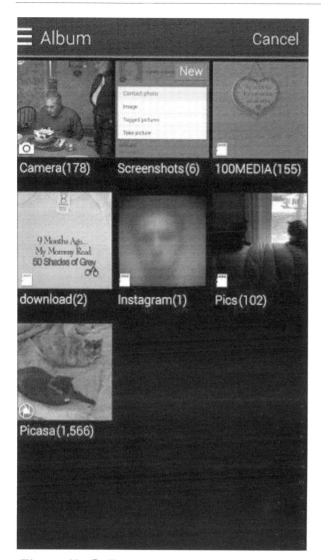

Figure 18: Gallery

14. Attaching a Video

The Galaxy S5 can send media messages containing videos. To attach a video to a text message:

1. Refer to *"Adding an Attachment to a Text Message"* on page 84 and follow steps 1-3. The Attachment menu appears.
2. Follow the steps in the appropriate section below:

Attaching a Video from the Camcorder

1. Touch the button. The camcorder turns on.

2. Touch the button. The video begins to record.

3. Touch the button. The camcorder stops recording and the preview screen appears.

4. Touch **Discard** to retake the video, or touch the icon in the center of the screen to preview it. The video plays.
5. Touch **Save**. The video is attached to the text message, as shown in **Figure 19**.

Note: The camcorder will automatically stop recording when the video has reached the maximum size limit.

Attaching a Video from the Videos Gallery (not recommended due to small size limit)

1. Touch the icon. A list of video albums appears.
2. Touch an album. The thumbnails of the videos in the album appear.
3. Touch a video. The video is attached to the text message.

*Note: If the message "File size too large" appears, try attaching a shorter video, or touch **Resize** to have the phone resize the video for you. Automatic resizing will not trim the video, but the quality will be drastically lower.*

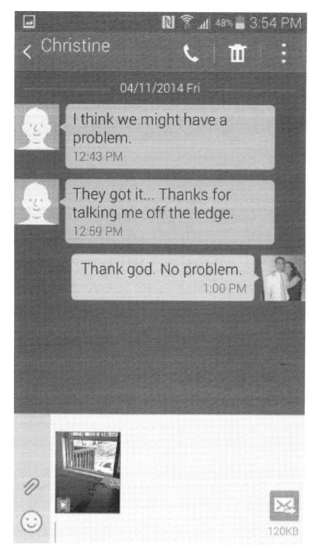

Figure 19: Text Message with Video Attached

15. Attaching a Voice Recording

The Galaxy S5 can send media messages containing voice recordings. To attach a voice recording to a text message:

1. Refer to *"Adding an Attachment to a Text Message"* on page 84 and follow steps 1-3. The Attachment menu appears.

2. Touch the [icon] icon. The voice recorder turns on, as shown in **Figure 20**.

3. Touch the [icon] button. The phone starts recording.

4. Touch the [icon] button to stop recording. The Voice Recorder dialog appears.

5. Touch the recording to preview it, and then touch **Done** to attach the recording. The recording is attached to the text message, as shown in **Figure 21**. You can also touch the [icon] button at any time while recording to discard the file.

Figure 20: Voice Recorder

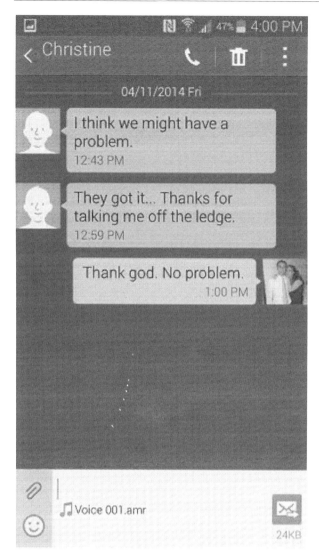

Figure 21: Text Message with Voice Recording Attached

16. Attaching a Memo

The Galaxy S5 can send a media message containing a memo. To attach a memo to a text message:

1. Refer to *"Adding an Attachment to a Text Message"* on page 84 and follow steps 1-3. The Attachment menu appears.

2. Touch the _____ icon. A list of memos appears, as shown in **Figure 22**. You can also touch the ⊕ icon to create a new memo.

3. Touch a memo in the list. The memo is attached to the text message, as shown in **Figure 23**.

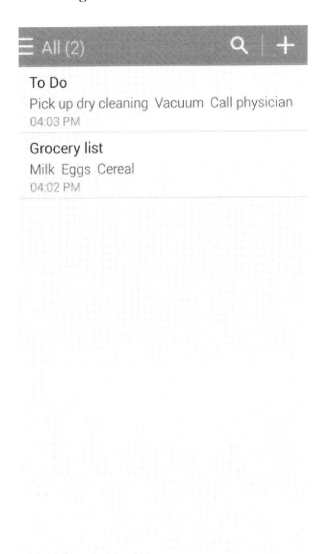

≡ All (2)   Q | +

To Do
Pick up dry cleaning Vacuum Call physician
04:03 PM

Grocery list
Milk Eggs Cereal
04:02 PM

Figure 22: List of Memos

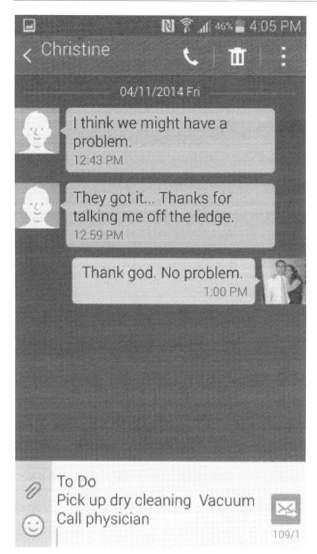

Figure 23: Text Message with Attached Memo

17. Attaching a Calendar Event

The Galaxy S5 can send a media message containing the information related to a calendar event, such as the date, time, and location. To attach a calendar event to a text message:

1. Refer to *"Adding an Attachment to a Text Message"* on page 84 and follow steps 1-3. The Attachment menu appears.

2. Touch the [31] icon. A list of events on your calendar appears, as shown in **Figure 24**.

3. Touch each event that you would like to attach. A ✓ appears next to each selected event.

4. Touch **Done** in the upper right-hand corner of the screen. The selected events are attached to the text message, as shown in **Figure 25** (with two events attached).

Note: No more than ten calendar events may be attached to a single text message.

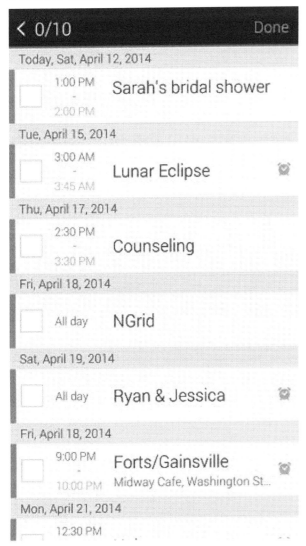

Figure 24: List of Events

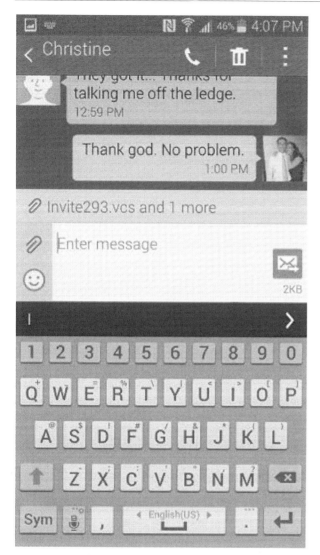

Figure 25: Text Message with Calendar Event Attached

18. Saving Attachments from Text Messages

After receiving an attachment in a text message, it can be saved to your Galaxy S5. To save an attachment from a text message:

1. Touch the ![icon] icon. The Messaging screen appears.
2. Touch a conversation. The conversation opens.
3. Touch and hold the attachment in the text message. The Message options appear.
4. Touch **Save attachment**. A list of files that are attached to the open conversation appears, as shown in **Figure 26**.

5. Touch an attachment to select it. A ✓ mark appears next to each selected attachment.
6. Touch **Save**. The attachment is saved to the Gallery.

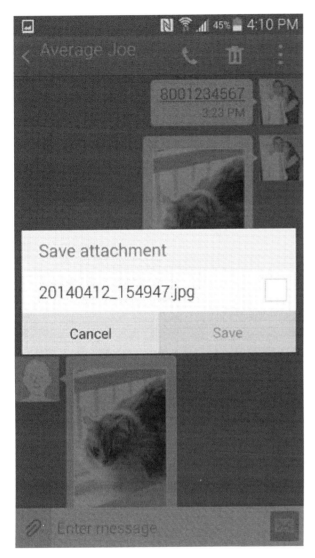

Figure 26: List of Attached Files

19. Sending a Text Message to an Entire Group

Creating contact groups allows you to send text messages to multiple people at a time without having to add each recipient separately. Refer to **Adding a Contact to a Group** to learn more about groups. To send a text to an entire group:

1. Touch the ![icon] icon at the bottom of the Home screen. The Messaging screen appears.

2. Touch the ![icon] icon in the upper right-hand corner of the screen. The New Message screen appears.

3. Touch the ![icon] button to the right of the 'Enter recipients' field. The Phonebook

4. Touch **Groups** in the upper right-hand corner of the screen. A list of groups appears, as shown in **Figure 27**. If you do not see 'Groups', touch Contacts and slide your finger to the left.

5. Touch the name of the group to which you would like to send a text message. A list of contacts that are contained in the group appears.

6. Touch **Select all**. All of the contacts in the group are selected, provided that there are ten contacts or less.

7. Touch **Done** in the upper right-hand corner of the screen. The selected contacts are added to the recipient field. Refer to *"Composing a New Text Message"* on page 67 to learn how to write and send a text message.

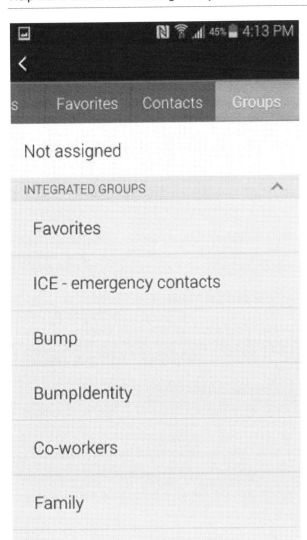

Figure 27: List of Groups

20. Managing Favorite Text Message Recipients

You may add contacts to a list of "Priority Senders", which are contacts that you text most often, in order to access them quickly when you're in a hurry.
To add favorite text message recipients:

1. Touch the ⬜ icon at the bottom of the Home screen. The Messaging screen appears.
2. Touch **Tap to add priority senders**, if this is the first time that you are adding a priority sender. The Priority Sender screen appears, as shown in **Figure 28**.
3. Touch **Contacts** to add contacts from your Phonebook, or touch **Inbox** to add contacts from your Messaging Inbox.
4. Touch the contacts or conversations that you wish to add to your priority sender list. A ✓ mark appears next to each selected contact or conversation.
5. Touch **Done** in the upper right-hand corner of the screen. The selected contacts are added to your priority list, which appears at the top of your Inbox, as outlined in **Figure 29**. To add more priority senders, touch the list and move your finger to the left until you see the ⊕ icon. Touch the ⊕ icon to add more contacts to the list.
6. Touch a contact in the Priority Sender list. A New Message screen appears with the contact's number already entered in the recipient field.

To remove a favorite text message recipient:

1. Touch and hold any contact in the Priority Sender list. The Priority Sender options appear, as shown in **Figure 30**.
2. Touch **Manage priority senders**. The ⊖ icons appear next to each contact in the priority list.
3. Touch the ⊖ icon next to a contact. The contact is removed from the list.
4. Touch **Done** in the upper right-hand corner of the screen. The priority list is saved. Alternatively, touch **Cancel** to discard your changes and replace the contacts that you just deleted.

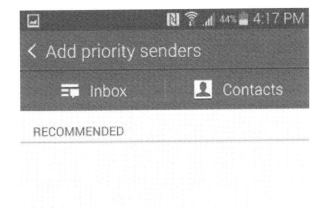

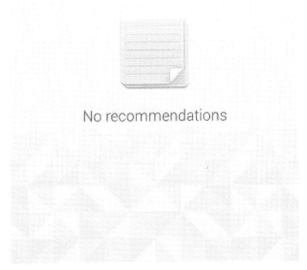

Figure 28: Priority Sender Screen

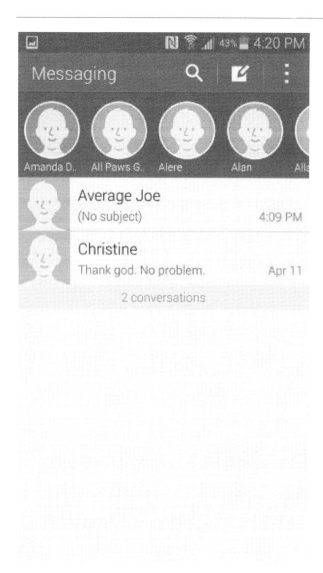

Figure 29: Priority List

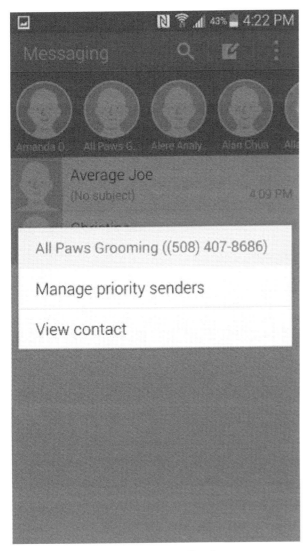

Figure 30: Priority Sender Options

Taking Pictures and Capturing Videos

Table of Contents

1. Taking a Picture
2. Using the Digital Zoom
3. Using Both Cameras at Once
4. Using the Flash
5. Applying an Effect before Taking a Picture
6. Setting the Camera Mode
7. Creating an Animated Photo
8. Creating a Panoramic Photo
9. Capturing a Video
10. Taking a Picture while Capturing a Video
11. Setting the Camcorder Mode
12. Editing Camera and Camcorder Settings

1. Taking a Picture

The Galaxy S5 has a rear-facing 16 megapixel camera with auto focus and a front-facing 2.1 megapixel camera. To take a picture, touch the icon. The camera turns on, as shown in **Figure 1**. Touch the icon to switch cameras. Touch a part of the screen to make the camera focus on that location. Touch the button. The picture is captured, and stored in the 'Camera' album.

Figure 1: Camera Turned On

2. Using the Digital Zoom

While taking pictures, use the camera's built-in Digital Zoom feature if the subject of the photo is far away. Digital Zoom can also be used while recording a video. To zoom in, touch the screen with two fingers and move them apart. To zoom out, touch the screen with two fingers spread apart and move them together.

Note: Because of its digital nature, the zoom function will not provide the best resolution, and the image may look fuzzy. It is recommended to be as close as possible to the subject of the photo or video.

3. Using Both Cameras at Once

The Galaxy S5 has a unique feature that allows you to take two pictures at once using the front and rear cameras at the same time. To use both cameras at once:

1. Touch the ⬤ icon. The camera turns on.
2. Touch **Mode** at the bottom of the screen. A list of modes appears, as shown in **Figure 2**.
3. Scroll down and touch **Dual camera**. A stamp appears in the upper left-hand corner and the front camera turns on, as shown in **Figure 3**.
4. Touch the stamp and move it to the desired location on the screen. You can also resize it by touching one of the corners and moving your finger.
5. Touch the ◣◥ icon at the bottom of the screen to replace the stamp with another shape. A list of available front camera shapes appears, as shown in **Figure 4**. Touch a shape to select it.
6. Touch the 📷 button. The picture is captured and stored in the 'Camera' album.

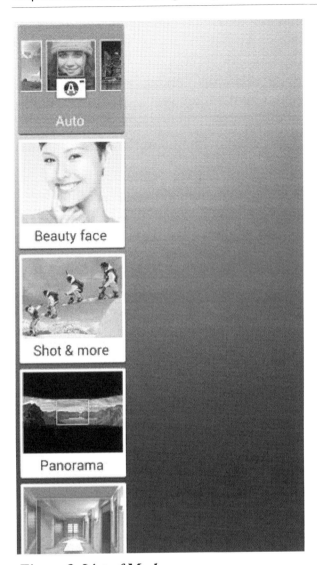

Figure 2: List of Modes

Figure 3: Front Camera Stamp

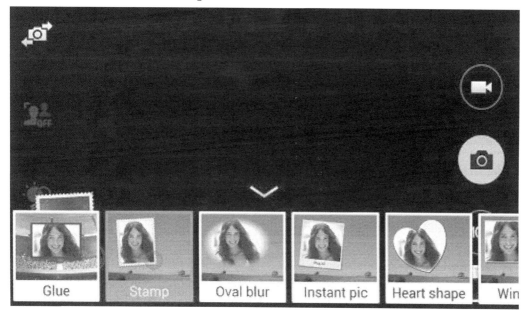

Figure 4: Front Camera Shapes

4. Using the Flash

The Galaxy S5 has a built-in flash, which can be used along with the rear-facing camera. When shooting a video with the flash turned on, it will remain on. To use the flash:

1. Touch the ⬛ icon. The camera turns on.

2. Touch the ⬛ icon. The Camera Settings appear, as shown in **Figure 5**.

3. Touch the ⬛ icon. The flash is turned on and will be used every time a picture is taken.

4. Touch the ⬛ icon. The flash is set to automatic and the surrounding light determines whether it is used.

5. Touch the ⬛ icon. The flash is turned off and will not be used when you are taking pictures.

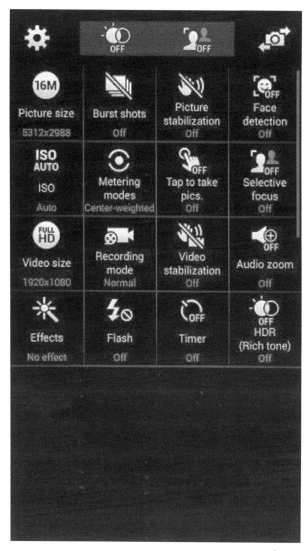

Figure 5: Camera Settings

5. Applying an Effect before Taking a Picture

In order to avoid having to apply an effect after taking a picture, you may apply certain simple effects before taking one. To apply an effect before taking a picture:

1. Touch the ![icon] icon. The Camera Settings appear.

2. Touch the ![icon] icon. A list of camera effects appears, as shown in **Figure 6**.

3. Touch the ![icon] icon at the bottom of the screen. Touch an effect in the list. A preview of the effect appears when you point the camera at the subject, as shown in **Figure** 7, where the Cartoon effect has been applied.

4. Touch the ![button] button. A picture is captured with the selected effect applied to it.

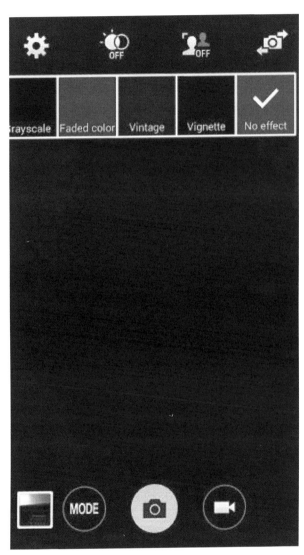

Figure 6: Camera Effects

Figure 7: Cartoon Effect

6. Setting the Camera Mode

You may wish to set a different camera mode depending on the environment, such as when taking a picture at night or at a sporting event. To set the camera mode, touch **Mode** at the bottom of the screen. The Camera Mode list appears. Touch a mode in the list. The selected mode is turned on. A description of each mode appears when you view it. You can also touch **Download** to install more camera modes.

7. Creating an Animated Photo

The camera allows you to create pictures that have animated elements, such as people or animals performing stunts. To create an animated photo:

1. Touch **Mode** at the bottom of the screen. A list of camera modes appears.
2. Touch **Download**. A list of downloadable modes appears, as shown in **Figure 8**.
3. Touch **Animated Photo**. A description of the mode appears.
4. Touch **Free**. The App Permissions appear. You may need to sign in to your Samsung account, or create one if you do not yet have a Samsung account.
5. Touch **Accept and download**. The Animated Photo mode is downloaded. Return to the camera by touching the key.
6. Select the **Animated Photo** mode. Refer to *"Setting the Camera Mode"* on page 113 to learn how.
7. Touch the button. The camera analyzes the scene, searching for moving objects. Hold the phone steady while analyzing. The Animation Editing screen appears, as shown in **Figure 9**.
8. Touch **Freeze** at the top of the screen and then select the part of the screen that you would like to keep from animating.
9. Touch **Done** in the upper right-hand corner of the screen. The animated photo is saved in the 'Camera' album.

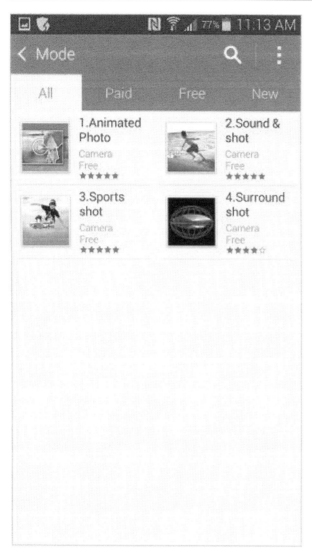

Figure 8: List of Downloadable Modes

Figure 9: Animation Editing Screen

8. Creating a Panoramic Photo

The camera allows you to take pictures of panoramic scenes that are too wide to fit in a normal picture, such as a landscape. To create a panoramic photo:

1. Select the **Panoramic** mode. Refer to *"Setting the Camera Mode"* on page 113 to learn how.

2. Move the camera the left-most part of the scene that you wish to capture. Touch the button. The camera captures the first frame, as shown in **Figure 10**.

3. Slowly move the camera to the right-most part of the scene. When the camera has finished capturing as much as it can store, the photo is automatically stored in the 'Camera' album.

Figure 10: First Frame of a Panoramic Photo

9. Capturing a Video

The Galaxy S5 has a built-in camcorder that allows you to capture videos. To capture a video:

1. Touch the ⬤ icon. The camera turns on.

2. Touch the ⬤ button. The camcorder begins to record video, as shown in **Figure 11**.

3. Touch the ⬤ button at any time to pause the camcorder. Touch the ⬤ button to resume recording.

4. Touch the ⬤ button. The camcorder stops recording, and the video is stored in the 'Camera' album.

Figure 11: Camcorder Recording a Video

10. Taking a Picture while Capturing a Video

While capturing a video, you may take a quick snapshot of the screen. To take a picture while

capturing a video, touch the ⬤ button. A photo is taken, and stored in the 'Camera' album.

11. Setting the Camcorder Mode

You may wish to set a different camcorder mode depending on your preferences, such as when attaching a video to a text message. To set the camcorder mode:

1. Touch the ⬤ icon. The camera turns on.
2. Touch the ⚙ icon. The Camera Settings appear.
3. Touch **Recording Mode** at the top of the screen. The Recording Mode menu appears, as shown in **Figure 12**.
4. Touch one of the following options to select the corresponding mode:

- **Normal** - Default recording mode with no effects.
- **Limit for MMS** - Limits the size of the video so that it can be attached to a text message.
- **Slow motion** - Makes the moving objects in the video move at a slower rate.
- **Fast motion** - Makes the moving objects in the video move at a faster rate.
- **Smooth motion** - Reduces the blurring effects of jerky movements while capturing a video.

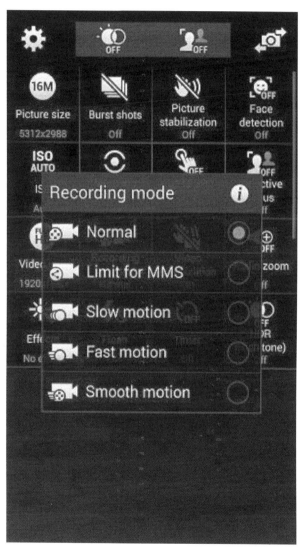

Figure 12: Recording Mode Menu

12. Editing Camera and Camcorder Settings

The camera and camcorder settings on the phone can be adjusted to essentially edit a photo or video before it is taken. Settings include changing the brightness, adding an effect, or changing the image quality.

Adjusting Camera Settings

To adjust the camera settings when the camera is turned on:

1. Touch the ![icon] icon. The Camera settings appear.
2. Touch one of the following to adjust the corresponding setting:

   - **Picture size** - Set the resolution of the photo. A higher resolution will produce a higher quality photo, but will take up more memory.
   - **Burst Shots** - Quickly takes several photos of a moving target.
   - **Picture Stabilization** - Allows the camera to capture higher quality pictures in the dark without the use of a flash.
   - **Face Detection** - Allows the camera to automatically detect and focus on people's faces.
   - **Metering modes** - Determines how the camera measures light. Center-weighted metering measures background light in the center of the scene. Spot metering measures light around the subject of the photo. Matrix metering averages the light in the entire scene.
   - **Tap to take pics** - Allows you to touch the screen anywhere to take a picture instead of having to touch the ![button] button.
   - **ISO** - Controls the camera's sensitivity to light. Use lower values for subjects that are not moving or those that are already brightly lit. Use higher values for subjects that are moving quickly or those that are poorly lit.
   - **Selective focus** - Allows the camera to focus on one particular object 1.5 feet or less away. The object is brought into the foreground, with all other elements of the photo slightly out of focus.
   - **Timer** - Delays the shot by the specified number of seconds.
   - **HDR (Rich tone)** - Allows the camera to take high quality pictures, which are created by taking several shots, averaging the amount of light in each, and then merging the photos into one. HDR photos are much larger in size than non-HDR ones.

Scroll down in the camera settings list to access the following settings:

- **Location tags** - Assigns a location to each photo that you take, provided that you have GPS services turned on.
- **Storage** - Determines where each captured photo is saved. Choose Memory card to store photos on a microSD card that you have inserted. Choose **Device** to store photos on the device's internal storage.
- **Review pics/videos** - Display a photo in the Gallery after it is taken. If 'Review' is turned on, you will need to navigate back to the camera every time that you take a picture.
- **Remote viewfinder** - Turns on the connected viewfinder to use in tandem with the S5 camera. Refer to the documentation provided with your viewfinder to learn how to connect it to the S5.
- **White balance** - Select the correct white balance to match the environment and create a true-to-life color range. The White Balance setting is similar to the Heat Range setting on professional cameras.
- **Exposure value** - Adjusts the amount of light that enters the camera's sensor. Use a higher exposure for low-light environments and vice versa.
- **Guide lines** - Activates gridlines to help you align the subjects in your shot.
- **Shutter sound** - Causes the phone to make a camera shutter sound every time a picture is taken.
- **Voice control** - Allows you to take pictures using voice commands, such 'Cheese' and 'Shoot'.
- **Reset** - Resets all camera and camcorder settings to factory defaults.

Adjusting Camcorder Settings

You may also adjust the following camcorder settings:

- **Video size** - Set the resolution of the video. A higher resolution will produce a higher quality video, but will take up more memory.
- **Video stabilization** - Prevents the motion blur that occurs when your hand shakes while capturing a video.
- **Audio zoom** - Focuses the phone's microphone on the subject of your video when you zoom in on that subject.

Managing Photo and Video Albums

Table of Contents

1. Browsing Photos and Videos
2. Starting a Slideshow
3. Editing a Photo
4. Tagging a Person in a Photo
5. Trimming a Video
6. Deleting Photos and Videos
7. Moving Photos between Albums
8. Creating a Photo Collage

1. Browsing Photos and Videos

You can browse pictures without activating the camera. To view saved images:

1. Touch the 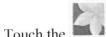 icon. The Gallery opens, as shown in **Figure 1**.

2. Touch an album. The album opens and the thumbnails of the photos in it appear, as shown in **Figure 2**.

3. Touch a photo or video. The photo appears in full-screen mode or the video begins to play.

4. Touch the screen and move your finger to the left or right. Other photos and videos in the same album appear.

5. Touch the button. The thumbnails of the pictures in the current album appear.

Figure 1: Gallery

Figure 2: Photo Thumbnails

2. Starting a Slideshow

The Galaxy S5 can play slideshows using the pictures stored in the Gallery. To start a slideshow:

1. Touch the ![icon] icon. The Gallery opens.
2. Touch an album. The album opens.
3. Touch and hold the ![key] key. The Album menu appears, as shown in **Figure 3**.
4. Touch **Slideshow**. The Slideshow Settings window appears, as shown in **Figure 4**.
5. Touch one of the following effects in the list to use it as a transition between photos during the slideshow:

   - **Flow** - No effect. Moves to the next photo by sliding the previous one horizontally to the left.
   - **Fade** - Slowly fades into the next photo while leaving the previous one on the screen.
   - **Zoom** - Slowly zooms into the current photo and then switches abruptly to the next one.
   - **Russian shuffle** - Keeps the next photo in the background, and then shuffles it to the front in a circular fashion.

6. Touch **Slideshow music** at the bottom of the Slideshow Settings window. Touch one of the options in the list to play music during the slideshow.
7. Touch a filter to apply a filter to every photo in the slideshow.
8. Touch the ![button] button in the upper right-hand corner of the screen. The slideshow begins.
9. Touch the screen anywhere. The slideshow ends and the photo album appears.

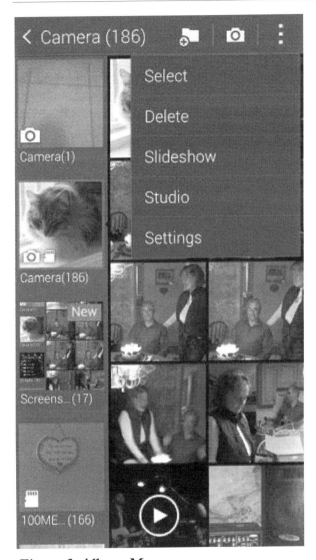

Figure 3: Album Menu

Figure 4: Slideshow Settings Window

3. Editing a Photo

After taking a picture, you can use the Galaxy S5 to crop it, rotate it, or enhance it with effects. To edit pictures in the Gallery:

1. Touch the ![icon] icon. The Gallery opens.
2. Touch an album. The album opens.
3. Touch a photo. The photo appears in full-screen mode.
4. Touch and hold the ![key] key. The Photo menu appears, as shown in **Figure 5**.
5. Touch **Edit**. The Photo Editing screen appears, as shown in **Figure 6**.
6. Follow the steps in one of the following sections to edit the photo:

Rotating a Photo

You may wish to rotate a photo to orient it vertically or horizontally. To rotate a photo:

1. Touch the ![icon] icon at the bottom of the screen. The Photo Adjustment menu appears, as shown in **Figure 7**.
2. Touch the ![icon] icon in the Photo Adjustment menu. Photo rotation is enabled.
3. Touch the photo and move your finger in a clockwise or counter-clockwise motion to rotate the photo accordingly. The photo is rotated.
4. You can also touch one of the following icons to rotate the photo accordingly:

![icon] - Rotates the photo 90 degrees counter-clockwise.

![icon] - Rotates the photo 90 degrees clockwise.

![icon] - Flips the photo 180 degrees to the left. This means that any objects pointing to the right will now point to the left, and vice versa.

![icon] - Flips the photo 180 degrees down. This means that any objects pointing down will now point up, and vice versa.

![icon] - Mirrors one half of the image. Touch the side of the image that you would like to mirror after touching this icon.

5. Touch **Done** in the upper right-hand corner of the screen when you are finished. The rotation is applied.

6. Touch the ![icon] icon in the upper right-hand corner of the screen. The quality menu appears, as shown in **Figure 8**.
7. Selecting a higher quality will result in a larger file. Select a quality level, and touch **OK**.
8. The photo is saved in the 'Studio' album. The original photo is left in its original location. Alternatively, touch **Cancel** at the top of the screen to discard the rotated photo and leave the original as it is.

Cropping a Photo

Crop a photo to use only a portion of it. To crop a photo:

1. Touch the ![icon] icon at the bottom of the screen. The Photo Adjustment menu appears.

2. Touch the ![icon] icon at the bottom of the screen. A white cropping rectangle appears on the photo. The portion of the photo that will be included in the crop is in color, while the rest is in black and white. If the photo is already in black and white, the previous sentence does not apply.

3. Use the following tips when cropping a photo:

   - Touch the ![icon] icons and drag them in any direction to change the size of the cropped area.
   - Touch inside the cropped area and move it to select the part of the photo that you wish to keep.
   - Touch one of the aspect ratio icons at the bottom of the screen, such as 1:1 or 16:9 to select a cropping rectangle with preset dimensions.

4. Touch **Done** in the upper right-hand corner of the screen when you are finished. The crop is applied to the photo.

5. Touch the ![icon] icon in the upper right-hand corner of the screen. The quality menu appears.

6. Selecting a higher quality will result in a larger file. Select a quality level, and touch **OK**.

7. The photo is saved in the 'Studio' album. The original photo is left in its original location. Alternatively, touch **Cancel** at the top of the screen to discard the cropped photo, and leave the original as it is.

Resizing a Photo

Resizing a photo allows you to change the file size as well as the actual size of the photo without distorting it in any way. To resize a photo:

1. Touch the ![icon] icon at the bottom of the screen. The Photo Adjustment menu appears.

2. Touch the ![icon] icon at the bottom of the screen. The photo appears in a white rectangle.

3. Touch and hold a ![icon] icon and drag it in any direction to resize the photo. The size of the photo is shown at the top of the screen. Touch **Done** when you are finished.

4. Touch the ![icon] icon in the upper right-hand corner of the screen. The quality menu appears.

5. Selecting a higher quality will result in a larger file. Select a quality level, and touch **OK**.

6. The photo is saved in the 'Studio' album. The original photo is left in its original location. Alternatively, touch **Cancel** at the top of the screen to discard the resized photo, and leave the original as it is.

Adjusting the Color Balance

You can manually adjust the color balance to achieve the desired appearance in a photo. To adjust the color balance:

1. Touch the ![icon] at the bottom of the screen. The Color Balance menu appears at the bottom of the screen, as shown in **Figure 9**.

2. Touch one of the following options to adjust the corresponding color setting. To adjust any of the settings, touch the photo anywhere, and then move your finger to the left or right to increase or decrease the effect, respectively.

   - **Contrast** - Increases or decreases the difference between the darkest and lightest areas of the photo.
   - **Brightness** - Adjust the brightness of the photo.
   - **Temperature** - Increases or decreases the amount of blue and white colors or red and yellow colors. A low temperature will produce a scene that imitates overcast conditions or winter, while a high temperature will produce a scene that looks like summer or a sunny day.
   - **Saturation** - Increases or decreases the difference between the colors in the photo. A minimum saturation will produce a black and white photo.
   - **Red** - Adjust the amount of red in the photo.
   - **Green** - Adjust the amount of green in the photo.
   - **Blue** - Adjust the amount of blue in the photo.
   - **Hue** - Adjusts the tint of the colors in the photo. This tool can completely alter the color of your photo.

3. Touch **Done** at the top of the screen. The color balance setting is saved when you are finished.

4. Touch the ⬛ icon in the upper right-hand corner of the screen. The quality menu appears.

5. Selecting a higher quality will result in a larger file. Select a quality level, and touch **OK**. The photo is saved as a copy of the original in the 'Studio' album. The original photo is left in its original location. Alternatively, touch **Cancel** at the top of the screen to discard the adjusted photo and leave the original as it is.

Adding Effects

To add special effects (such as vintage or sepia) to a photo:

1. Touch the ⬛ icon at the bottom of the screen. A list of effects appears, as shown in **Figure 10**.

2. Touch the desired effect. Some effects require adjustment. Touch **Done** at the top of the screen when you are finished. The effect is applied.

3. Touch the ⬛ icon. The quality menu appears. Selecting a higher quality will result in a larger file.

4. Select a quality level, and touch **OK**. The photo is saved as a copy of the original in the 'Studio' album. The original photo is left in its original location. Alternatively, touch **Cancel** at the top of the screen to discard the adjusted photo and leave the original as it is.

Touching Up Faces

You may wish to perform some touch up on the faces in a photo, especially for formal occasions. To touch up a face:

1. Touch the ⬛ icon at the bottom of the screen. The Portrait options appear at the bottom of the screen, as shown in **Figure 11**.

2. Touch one of the options below and then use the + and - to apply and adjust the corresponding effect:

   - **Remove red eye** - Removes red eyes from a photo. Touch an eye to remove the red-eye effect.
   - **Airbrush** - Removes imperfections, including pimples and even minor facial hair, from the entire face.
   - **Brighten face** - Increases or decreases the amount of light shed on a face.
   - **Out-of-focus** - Increases or decreases the focus on the background of the photo.

Figure 5: Photo Menu

Figure 6: Photo Editing Screen

Figure 7: Photo Adjustment Menu

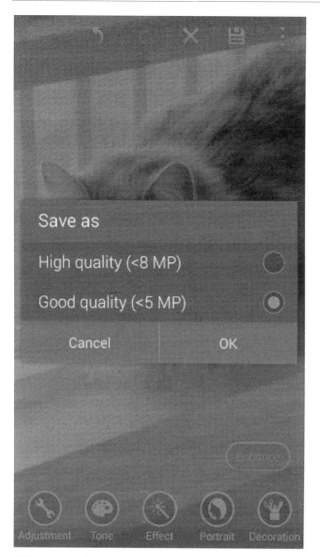

Figure 8: Quality Menu

Figure 9: Color Balance Menu

Figure 10: List of Effects

Figure 11: Portrait Options

4. Tagging a Person in a Photo

You may tag specific people in photos in order to find them more quickly. To tag a person in a photo:

1. Open a photo. Refer to *"Browsing Photos and Videos"* on page 122 to learn how.
2. Touch and hold the [image] key. The Photo menu appears.
3. Scroll down and touch **Settings**. The Gallery Settings screen appears, as shown in **Figure 12**.

4. Touch the box next to 'Face Tag'. A mark appears and Face Tagging is turned on. Touch the key to return to the photo.
5. Touch a face in the photo. A white rectangle appears around the face.
6. Touch anywhere inside the white rectangle. 'Add name' and 'Me' appears.
7. Touch **Me** if you wish to tag yourself. Otherwise, touch **Add name**. The Phonebook appears.
8. Touch the name of a contact. The face is tagged as the contact that you selected. If the contact does not exist in the Phonebook, touch the button to add him or her.

Figure 12: Gallery Settings Screen

5. Trimming a Video

You may trim a video in order to keep only the segment that you want. To trim a video:

1. Open the video. Refer to *"Browsing Photos and Videos"* on page 122 to learn how.
2. Touch the ✂ icon at the top of the screen. If you do not see the ✂ icon, touch the screen anywhere. The Video Trimming screen appears, as shown in **Figure 13**.
3. Touch the ┃ icon and drag it to the right to select the beginning of the video and cut out the rest of the content at the beginning. Touch the ┃ icon and drag it to the left to select the end of the video and cut out the rest of the content at the end.
4. Touch **Done** in the upper right-hand corner of the screen. The New File name dialog appears.
5. Enter a name for the new video and touch **OK**. The new video is saved as a copy in the same album.

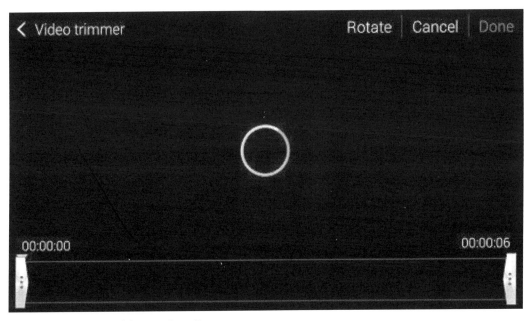

Figure 13: Video Trimming Screen

6. Deleting Photos and Videos

Warning: Once a photo or video is deleted, there is no way to restore it, so make sure that you do not want the selected files.

To free up some space in the phone's memory, try deleting photos or videos from the Gallery. To delete a photo or video:

1. Open a photo album. Refer to *"Browsing Photos and Videos"* on page 122 to learn how.
2. Touch and hold a photo or video. The photo is selected and a ✔ mark appears on it, as outlined in red in **Figure 14**.
3. Touch as many photos and videos as desired. The items are selected.
4. Touch the 🗑 icon in the upper right-hand corner of the screen. A confirmation dialog appears.
5. Touch **OK**. The selected items are deleted.

Figure 14: Selected Photos

7. Moving Photos between Albums

You may wish to organize your photos by moving them between albums. To move photos between albums:

1. Open a photo album. Refer to *"Browsing Photos and Videos"* on page 122 to learn how.

2. Touch and hold a photo or video. The photo is selected and a ✔ mark appears on it. Touch any other photos that you wish to move to another album.

3. Touch the button in the upper right-hand corner of the screen. The Album Management menu appears, as shown in **Figure 15**.

4. Touch **Move to album**. A list of available albums appears, as shown in **Figure 16**.
5. Touch an album. The photos and videos are moved to the selected album. You may also touch **Create new** to create a new album. Once the album is created, the photos are automatically moved to it.

Figure 15: Album Management Menu

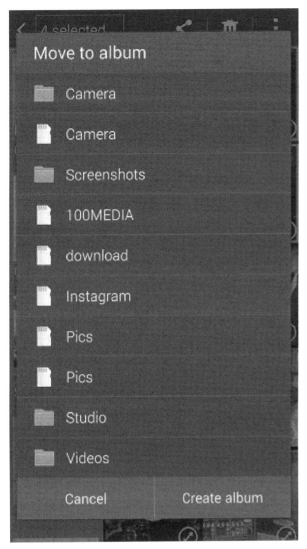

Figure 16: List of Available Albums

8. Creating a Photo Collage

A new feature on the Galaxy S 5 is the ability to create collages from your photos. To create a photo collage:

1. Open a photo album. Refer to *"Browsing Photos and Videos"* on page 122 to learn how.
2. Touch and hold a photo or video. The photo is selected and a ✓ mark appears on it. Touch any other photos that you wish to include in the collage. A maximum of six photos may be added.

3. Touch the ⋮ icon in the upper right-hand corner of the screen. The Album menu appears.
4. Touch **Studio**. A list of studios appears, as shown in **Figure 17**.
5. Touch **Collage studio**. The Collage Studio appears and the selected photos are added to the collage, as shown in **Figure 18**.
6. You may customize the Aspect ratio, layout, border, and background by touching the corresponding setting at the bottom of the screen.
7. Touch the ▤ icon at the top of the screen when you are finished. The quality menu appears. Selecting a higher quality will result in a larger file.
8. Select a quality level, and touch **OK**. The photo is saved as a copy of the original in the 'Studio' album.

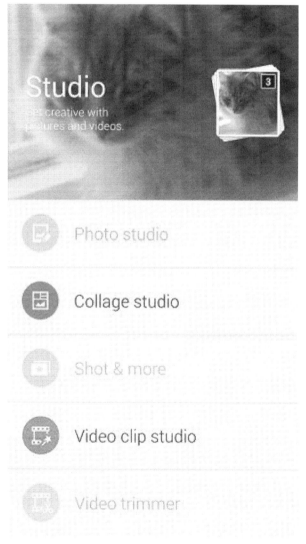

Figure 17: List of Studios

Figure 18: Collage Studio

Using the Chrome Web Browser

Table of Contents

1. Navigating to a Web Page
2. Adding and Viewing Bookmarks
3. Managing Browser Tabs
4. Working with Links
5. Searching a Web Page for a Word or Phrase
6. Viewing the Browsing History
7. Sharing a Web Page
8. Setting the Search Engine
9. Turning Autofill On or Off
10. Saving Passwords
11. Turning Pop-Up Blocking On or Off
12. Changing the Text Size
13. Clearing Personal Data

1. Navigating to a Web Page

You can surf the Web using your Galaxy S5. It is highly recommended that you use the Google Chrome browser for the best Web experience. To navigate to a Web page using a Web address, or URL:

1. Touch the icon, or touch the icon and then touch the icon. The Chrome browser opens, as shown in **Figure 1**.
2. Touch the address bar at the top of the screen, as outlined in **Figure 1**. The address is highlighted in blue and the virtual keyboard appears.
3. Enter the Web address and touch **Go** in the lower right-hand corner of the screen. The phone navigates to the corresponding Website.

Note: Refer to "Tips and Tricks" *on page 305 to learn more about using the address bar.*

147

Figure 1: Chrome Browser Open

2. Adding and Viewing Bookmarks

The Galaxy S5 can store favorite Web pages as bookmarks to allow you to access them faster in the future. To add a bookmark:

1. Navigate to a Web page. Refer to *"Navigating to a Web Page"* on page 147 to learn how.

2. Touch and hold the ![key icon] key. The Chrome menu appears, as shown in **Figure 2**.

3. Touch the ☆ icon. The Add Bookmark screen appears, as shown in **Figure 3**.

4. Enter a name for the bookmark and touch **Save**. The Web page is saved to your bookmarks. You can also save the bookmark to a specific folder by touching **Mobile bookmarks** and selecting a different folder.

To view saved bookmarks:

1. Touch and hold the 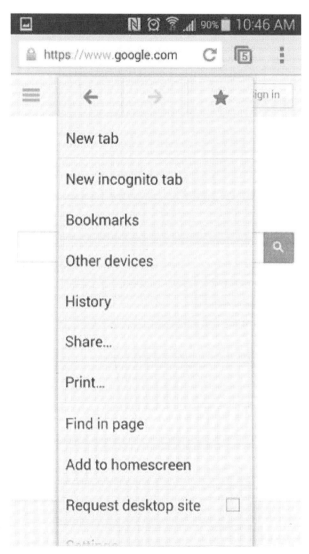 key. The Chrome menu appears.
2. Touch **Bookmarks**. A list of bookmarks appears, as shown in **Figure 4**.
3. Touch a bookmark. Chrome navigates to the Web page.

Figure 2: Chrome Menu

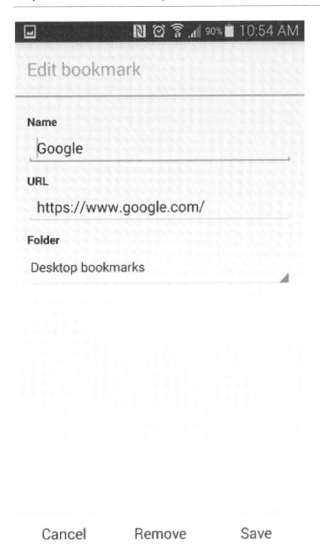

Figure 3: Add Bookmark Screen

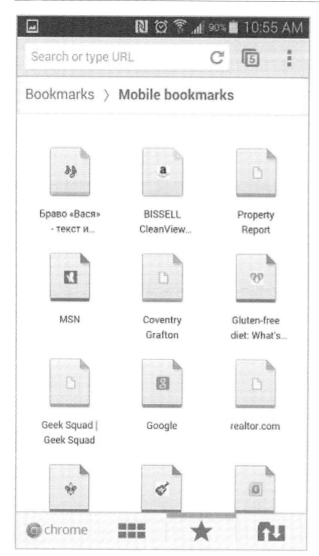

Figure 4: List of Bookmarks

3. Managing Browser Tabs

The Chrome browser supports an unlimited number of tabs. Use the following tips when working with open browser windows:

- Touch the ⬛ icon (the number on the icon varies depending on the number of tabs currently open). The open tabs appear, as shown in **Figure 5**.
- Touch **New Tab**. A new tab is created.

- Touch a tab while viewing all open tabs, and slide your finger to the left or right. The selected tab is closed.
- Touch a tab while viewing all open tabs. The tab opens.

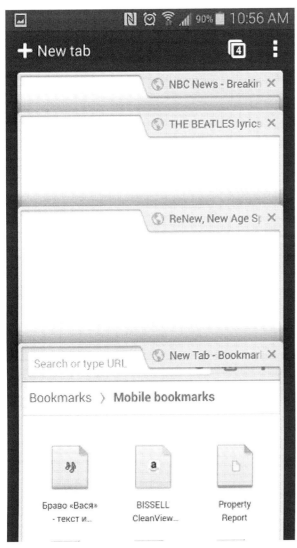

Figure 5: Open Tabs

4. Working with Links

In addition to touching a link to navigate to its destination, there are other link options. Touch and hold a link to see all link options, as shown in **Figure 6**. The following options are available:

- **Open in new tab** - Opens the link in a new tab, so as not lose the current Web page. Refer to *"Managing Browser Tabs"* on page 151 to learn how to view all open tabs.
- **Open in incognito tab** - Opens the link in a new incognito tab, so as not lose the current Web page. Any sites that you visit using the incognito tab are not recorded in your browsing history. Refer to *"Managing Browser Tabs"* on page 151 to learn how to view all open tabs.
- **Copy link address** - Copies the Web address to the clipboard. Touch and hold an empty space in any application and touch Paste to paste the link. Refer to *"Navigating to a Web Page"* on page 147 to learn how to visit a Website using the URL.
- **Copy link text** - Selects the text in the link to be copied and pasted in another location. Refer to *"Copying, Cutting, and Pasting Text"* on page 70 to learn more. You can also touch and hold plain text to achieve the same effect.
- **Save Link** - Downloads the Web page to the phone.

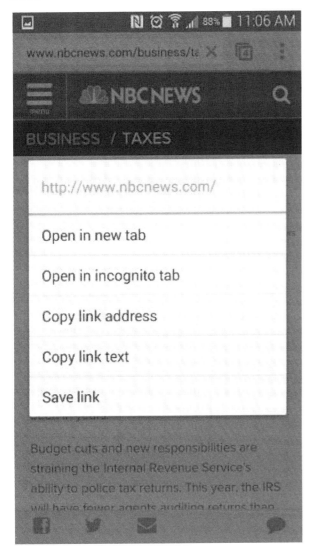

Figure 6: Link Options

5. Searching a Web Page for a Word or Phrase

While surfing the Web, any page can be searched for a word or phrase. To perform a search on a Web page:

1. Navigate to a Web page. Refer to *"Navigating to a Web Page"* on page 147 to learn how.
2. Touch and hold the ⬚ key. The Browser menu appears.
3. Touch **Find in page**. 'Find in page' appears at the top of the screen.

4. Enter the search term or phrase. The matching results are highlighted in orange and yellow on the Web page as you type, as shown in **Figure 7**. Alternatively, 0/0 appears at the top of the screen if no matches are found.

5. Touch the ∧ or ∨ arrow to select the previous or next matching result, respectively. The currently selected result is highlighted in orange.

6. Touch the 🔍 key. The virtual keyboard is hidden so that you can review the search results.

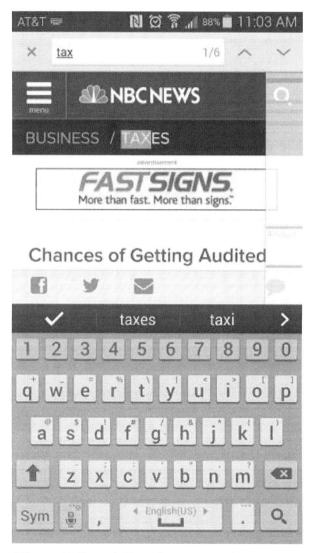

Figure 7: Search Results on a Web Page

6. Viewing the Browsing History

The Galaxy S5 stores all recently visited Web pages in its Browsing History. Since Chrome will match a Web address as you type, you will rarely need to manually view the history. To view the Browsing History while using the Chrome browser:

1. Touch the address bar at the top of the screen. The Web address is highlighted in blue.
2. Enter **chrome:history**. The Browsing History appears, as shown in **Figure 8**.
3. Touch a Web page in the list. Chrome navigates to the selected Web page.

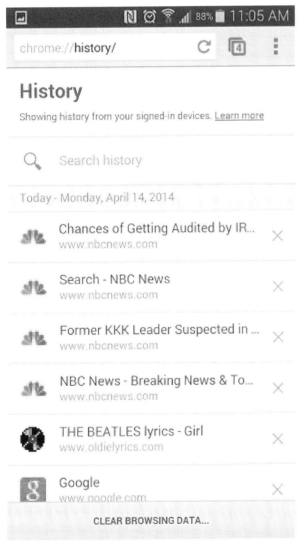

Figure 8: Browsing History

7. Sharing a Web Page

If you find a particularly interesting Web page, you can share it with a friend. To share a Web page:

1. Navigate to the Web page. Refer to Navigating to a Web Page to learn how.
2. Touch and hold the ▢ key. The Browser menu appears.

3. Touch **Share**. The Web Page Sharing menu appears, as shown in **Figure 9**.
4. Touch an option in the list to share the Web page. When sharing it via Email or Text Message, you will need to enter the recipient's address or phone number, respectively. When sharing it via a social application, such as Flipboard or Google+, you will need to login before you can share.

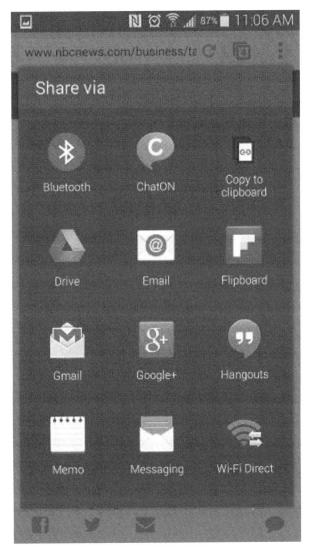

Figure 9: Web Page Sharing Menu

8. Setting the Search Engine

By default, the Chrome browser uses Google as the search engine. To perform a search, enter the search terms in the address bar at the top of the screen and touch the **Go** button. To set the search engine that is used when you perform a search:

1. Touch and hold the ▭ key. The Browser menu appears.
2. Scroll down and touch **Settings**. The Chrome Settings screen appears, as shown in **Figure 10**.
3. Touch **Search engine**. A list of available search engines appears.

4. Touch the search engine that you prefer. The selected search engine will be used every time you perform a search from the address bar.

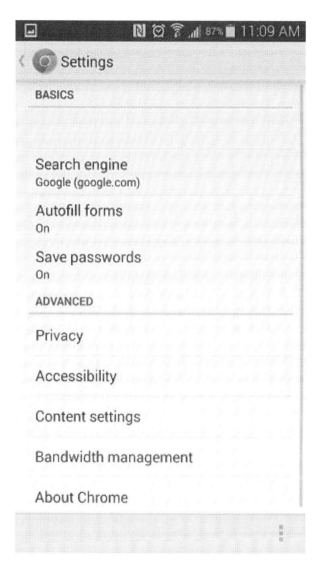

Figure 10: Chrome Settings Screen

9. Turning Autofill On or Off

Chrome can automatically fill in certain personal information to save you time. By default, Autofill is turned on. To turn Autofill on or off:

Warning: Using Autofill to enter personal information may be dangerous, as hackers may gain access to your credentials and use them to steal your identity. Always use strong passwords with a combination of numbers, letters, and symbols.

1. Touch and hold the ▣ key. The Browser menu appears.
2. Touch **Settings**. The Chrome Settings screen appears.
3. Touch **Autofill forms**. The Autofill Profiles screen appears, as shown in **Figure 11**.
4. Touch **Add profile**. The Add Profile screen appears, as shown in **Figure 12**.
5. Enter your personal information. Scroll down and touch **Save** when you are finished. The new profile is saved. You can also add credit card information by repeating this process and touching **Add credit card** in step 4.
6. Touch the ON switch in the upper right-hand corner of the screen if you wish to stop using Autofill. Autofill is turned off.

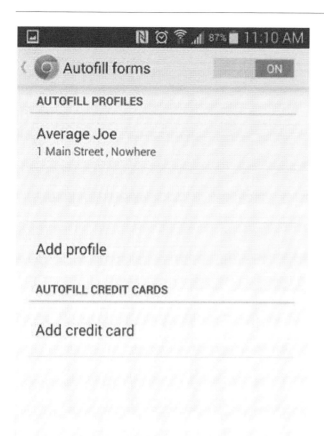

Figure 11: Autofill Profiles Screen

Figure 12: Add Profile Screen

10. Saving Passwords

Chrome can save passwords for you in order to save time when logging in to protected services. When this feature is turned on, the Password Saving dialog will appear every time that you enter a password, as shown in **Figure 13**. By default, this feature is turned on. To turn password saving on or off:

Warning: Using saved passwords may be dangerous, as hackers may gain access to your credentials and use them to steal your identity. Always use strong passwords with a combination of numbers, letters, and symbols.

1. Touch and hold the 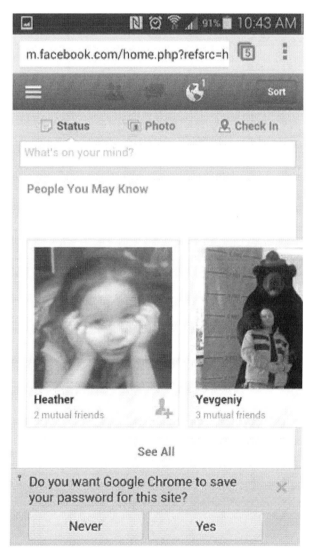 key. The Browser menu appears.
2. Touch **Settings**. The Chrome Settings screen appears.
3. Touch **Save passwords**. The Saved Passwords screen appears, as shown in **Figure 14**.
4. Touch the ON switch in the upper right-hand corner of the screen. Saving Passwords is turned off and Chrome will no longer offer to save any passwords.
5. Touch the OFF switch in the upper right-hand corner of the screen. Saving Passwords is turned on.

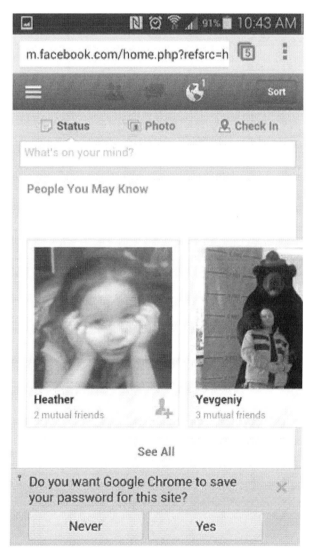

Figure 13: Password Saving Dialog

Figure 14: Saved Passwords Screen

11. Turning Pop-Up Blocking On or Off

Some Web pages may cause annoying pop-ups to appear. Chrome can automatically prevent these pop-ups from appearing. However, some sites may need to open additional pages in new tabs. For this reason, you may wish to turn the pop-up blocker off. By default, the pop-up blocker is turned on. To turn pop-up blocking on or off:

1. Touch and hold the ⬜ key. The Browser menu appears.

2. Touch **Settings**. The Chrome Settings screen appears.

3. Touch **Content settings**. The Content Settings screen appears, as shown in **Figure 15**.

4. Touch **Block pop-ups**. The ☑ mark disappears, and Chrome will no longer block any pop-ups

5. Touch **Block pop-ups** again. The ☑ mark appears, and Chrome will block all pop-ups.

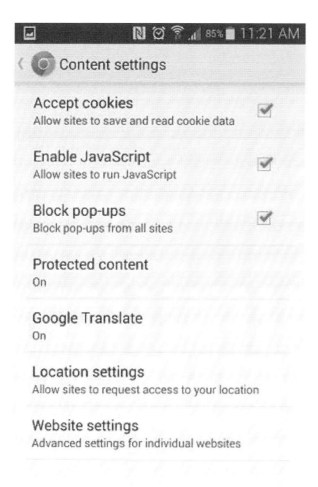

Figure 15: Content Settings Screen

12. Changing the Text Size

If you have trouble seeing small text in Chrome, you may wish to increase the text size. On the other hand, if you wish to see more text on a single screen, you may wish to decrease its size. To change the text size:

1. Touch and hold the ![key] key. The Browser menu appears.
2. Touch **Settings**. The Chrome Settings screen appears.
3. Touch **Accessibility**. The Chrome Accessibility Settings screen appears, as shown in **Figure 16**.

4. Touch the ![slider] slider below 'Text scaling' and drag it to the left to decrease the text size, or to the right to increase it. The text size is adjusted accordingly, and a preview of the actual size of the text in the Chrome browser is shown above 'Text scaling'.

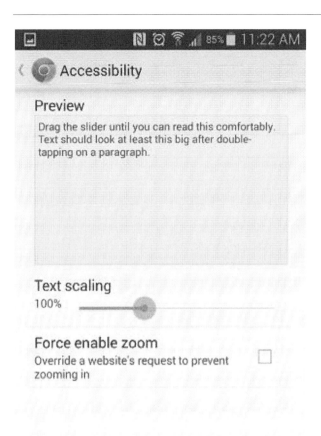

Figure 16: Chrome Accessibility Settings Screen

13. Clearing Personal Data

In order to protect your privacy, Chrome can clear your personal data, such as the list of recently visited Websites, known as the History. The phone can also clear other data, such as saved passwords and Autofill forms. To clear personal data while using the Chrome browser:

1. Touch and hold the ▣ key. The Browser menu appears.
2. Touch **Settings**. The Chrome Settings screen appears.
3. Touch **Privacy**. The Privacy Settings screen appears, as shown in **Figure 17**.
4. Touch **CLEAR BROWSING DATA** at the bottom of the screen. The Clear Browsing Data window appears, as shown in **Figure 18**.
5. Touch one or more of the following options to select the data that you wish to erase:

   - **Clear browsing history** - Deletes all history files, which include the addresses of recently visited Websites.
   - **Clear the cache** - Deletes all Web page data, such as image files and other files that comprise a Web page.
   - **Clear cookies, site data** - Deletes all text data, such as site preferences, authentication, or shopping cart contents.
   - **Clear saved passwords** - Deletes all stored passwords for various Websites, such as online email clients, marketplaces, and banking clients.
   - **Clear autofill data** - Deletes all form data, such as screen names, addresses, and phone numbers.

6. Touch **Clear**. The selected data is permanently erased.

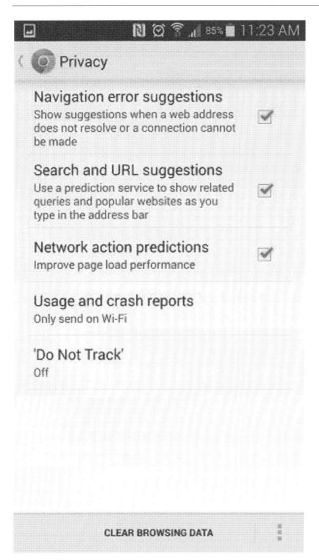

Figure 17: Privacy Settings Screen

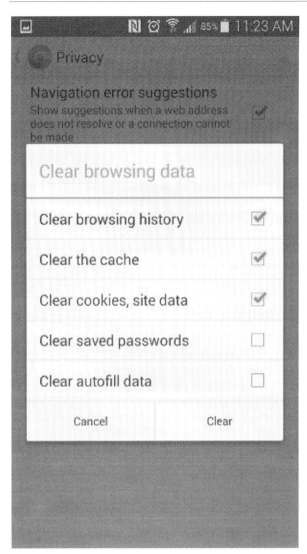

Figure 18: Clear Browsing Data Window

Using the Email Application

Table of Contents

1. Adding an Email Account to the Phone
2. Reading Email
3. Sending an Email
4. Replying to and Forwarding Emails
5. Deleting Emails and Restoring Deleted Emails to the Inbox
6. Searching the Inbox
7. Blocking All Emails from a Specific Sender

1. Adding an Email Account to the Phone

Before using the Email application, add at least one Email account to the Galaxy S5. To add an email account to the phone:

1. Touch the ![icon] icon, or touch the ![icon] icon and then touch the ![icon] icon. The first time that you open the Email application, the Email Account screen appears, as shown in **Figure 1**.
2. Enter your email address and password, and touch **Next**. The Account Options screen appears, as shown in **Figure 2**.
3. Touch **2 weeks** to select how far back email should be synced on your phone. Touch **Every hour** to select how often email will be synced to your phone.
4. Touch **Next** when you are finished. The Account Name screen appears, as shown in **Figure 3**.
5. Enter an optional name for the account, and touch **Done**. The account setup is complete.

Figure 1: Email Account Screen

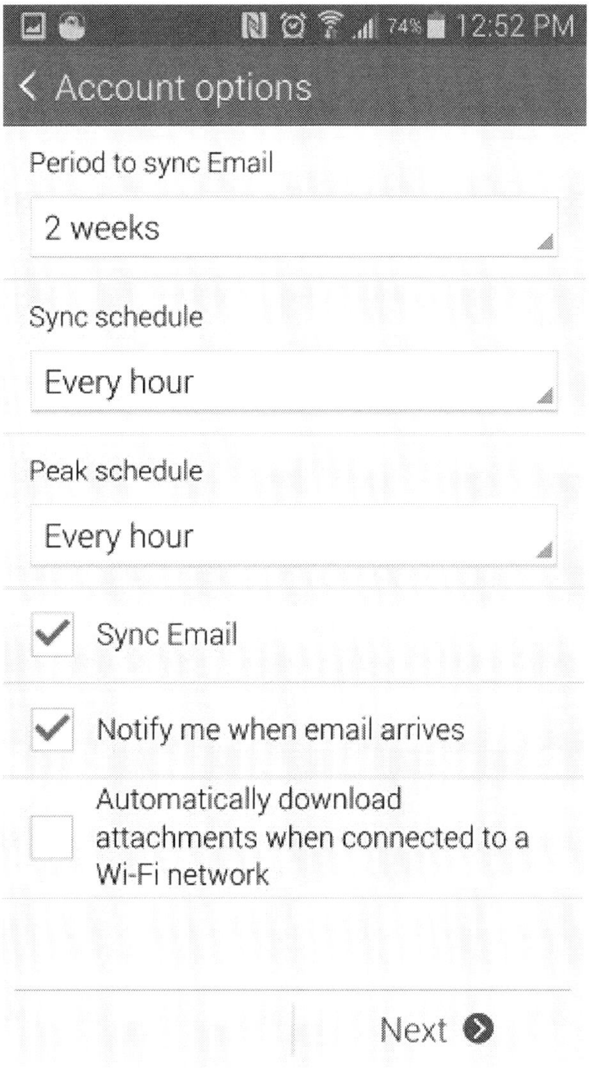

Figure 2: Account Options

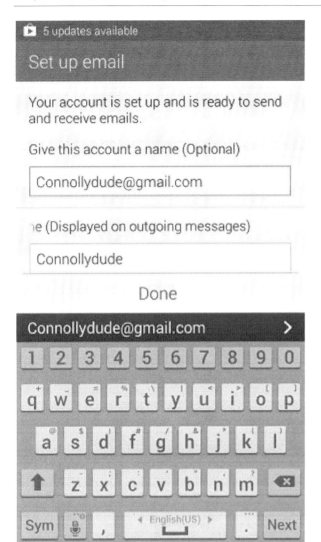

Figure 3: Account Name Screen

2. Reading Email (Email App)

You can read your email on the Galaxy S5 using the Email application. To read email:

1. Touch the 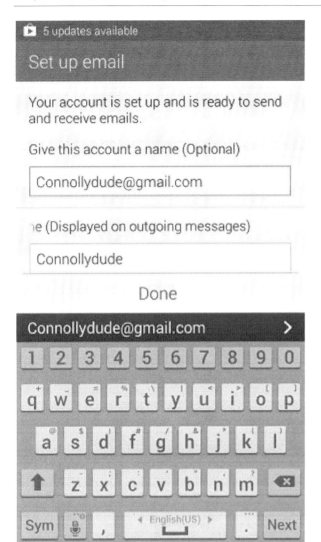 icon, or touch the icon and then touch the icon. The Inbox appears, as shown in **Figure 4**.
2. Touch an email in the list. The email opens.
3. Touch the screen and move your finger to the left or right to view the previous or next email, respectively. The email appears.

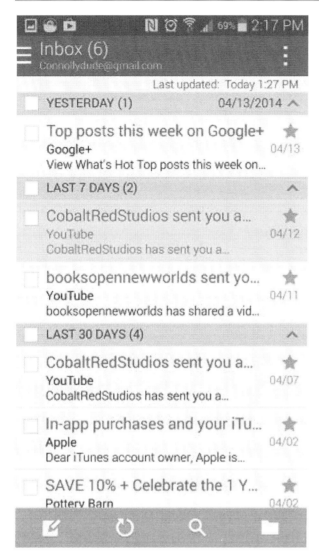

Figure 4: Email Inbox

3. Sending an Email (Email App)

Compose email directly from the Galaxy S5 using the Email application. To write an email while using the Email application:

1. Open the Inbox. Refer to *"Reading Email (Email App)"* on page 189 to learn how.

2. Touch the [icon] icon. The Compose screen appears, as shown in **Figure 5**.

3. Start typing the name of a contact for whom you have a saved email address. A list of suggestions appears.
4. Touch the contact's name. The contact's email address is inserted. Alternatively, you may type an email from scratch in the 'To' field.
5. Touch **Subject** and enter an optional topic for the email. Touch the white space below 'Subject' and enter a message. The subject and message are entered.
6. Touch the 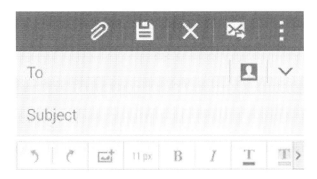 button in the upper right-hand corner of the screen. The email is sent.

Figure 5: Compose Screen

4. Replying to and Forwarding Emails (Email App)

After receiving an email, you can reply to the sender or forward the email to a new recipient. To reply to, or forward, an email while using the Email application:

1. Open the Inbox. Refer to *"Reading Email (Email App)"* on page 174 to learn how.
2. Touch an email. The email opens.
3. Touch the ![icon] icon at the bottom of the screen, as outlined in **Figure 6**. A new email is generated with the sender's email address already entered in the 'To' field.
4. Enter a message and touch the ![icon] button. The reply is sent.
5. Alternatively, touch the ![icon] icon or the ![icon] icon to the right of the ![icon] icon in step 3.

   Choosing 'Reply all' (![icon]) will send a reply to all recipients of the original email.

   Choosing 'Forward' (![icon]) will send a copy of the message to a different recipient, requiring you to enter an email address in the 'To' field. Follow step 4 to reply to all recipients, or to forward the email.

Figure 6: Reply Icon Outlined

5. Deleting Emails and Restoring Deleted Emails to the Inbox (Email App)

Deleting an email sends it to the Trash folder. To completely delete an email, the Trash folder must be emptied. To delete emails while using the Email application:

Warning: Emails in the Trash folder are permanently deleted after 30 days. Make sure that you retrieve the message before 30 days if you still need it.

1. Open the Inbox. Refer to *"Reading Email (Email App)"* on page 174 to learn how.

2. Touch the ☐ box to the left of the email that you wish to delete. A ✔ mark appears next to the selected email. Touch any additional emails that you wish to delete.

3. Touch the 🗑 icon at the bottom of the screen. The emails are sent to the 'Trash' folder.

To restore deleted emails to the Inbox:

1. Open the Inbox. Refer to *"Reading Email (Email App)"* on page 174 to learn how.
2. Touch **Inbox** in the upper left-hand corner of the screen. A list of the most frequent email folders appears.
3. Touch **Show all folders**. A list of all email folders appears, as shown in **Figure 7**.
4. Touch **Trash**. The Trash folder appears.

5. Touch the ☐ box to the left of the email that you wish to restore. A ✔ mark appears next to the selected email. Touch any additional emails that you wish to restore.

6. Touch the 📇 icon at the bottom of the screen. The Move menu appears, as shown in **Figure 8**.

7. Touch **Inbox**. The selected emails are restored to the Inbox.

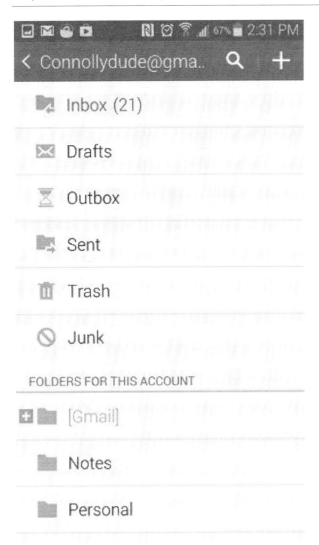

Figure 7: List of Email Folders

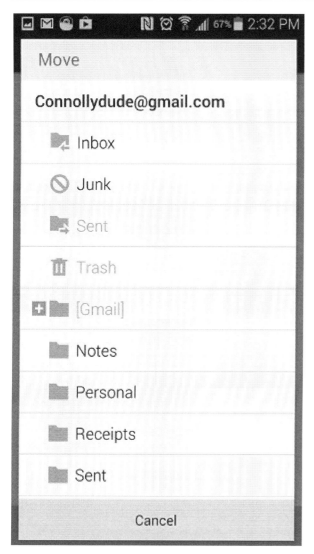

Figure 8: Move Menu

6. Searching the Inbox (Email App)

To find an email in the Inbox, use the search function, which searches email addresses, message content, and subject lines. To search the Inbox while using the Email application:

1. Open the Inbox. Refer to *"Reading Email (Email App)"* on page 174 to learn how.

2. Touch the 🔍 icon at the bottom of the screen. The virtual keyboard appears.

3. Enter a search word or phrase and touch **Done**. The Galaxy S5 searches the Inbox and a list of matching results appears.

7. Blocking All Emails from a Specific Sender

If you receive unwanted emails from the same email address, such as a solicitor of unwanted products or services, you may block the sender altogether by marking the email as 'Spam'. To block emails from a specific sender:

1. Open the Inbox. Refer to *"Reading Email (Email App)"* on page 174 to learn how.

2. Touch the ☐ box to the left of the email whose sender you wish to block. A ✓ mark appears next to the selected email. Touch any additional emails whose senders you wish to block.

3. Touch the icon at the bottom of the screen. The Spam menu appears, as shown in **Figure 9**.

4. Touch **Block the sender**. The selected emails and all future emails from the selected senders will be moved directly to the Spam folder. You may also touch **Block the domain** to block any emails that end with @NAME.com, such as "@aol.com."

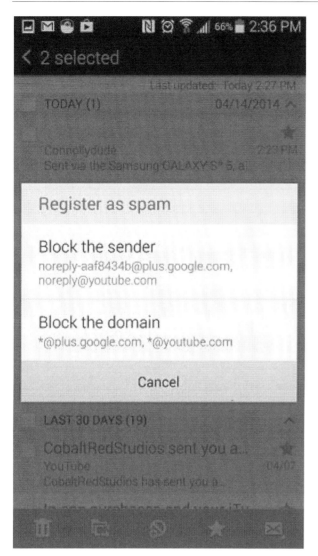

Figure 9: Spam Menu

Using the Gmail Application

Table of Contents

1. Adding a Google Account to the Phone
2. Reading Email
3. Sending an Email
4. Replying to and Forwarding Emails
5. Deleting Emails and Restoring Deleted Emails to the Inbox
6. Adding Labels to Emails
7. Searching the Inbox
8. Ignoring New Messages in a Conversation
9. Blocking All Emails from a Specific Sender
10. Adjusting the General Gmail Preferences
11. Adjusting Gmail Account Preferences

1. Adding a Google Account to the Phone

Before using the Gmail application, add at least one Google account to the Galaxy S5. It is highly recommended to use the Gmail service with the phone, since a Gmail account is required to use the application store (Play Store) anyway. To add a Google account to the phone:

1. Touch the top of the screen and drag it down. The Notifications screen appears, as shown in **Figure 1**.

2. Touch the icon in the upper right-hand corner of the screen. The Settings screen appears, as shown in **Figure 2**.

3. Scroll down and touch the icon under the 'User and Backup' section. The Accounts screen appears, as shown in **Figure 3**.

4. Touch **Add account**. The Add Account screen appears, as shown in **Figure 4**.

5. Touch **Google**. The Add Google Account screen appears, as shown in **Figure 5**.

6. Touch **New** at the bottom of the screen if you do not yet have a Google account. Enter all of the required information on the following screens to create your account. Otherwise, touch **Existing** and enter your Google credentials to login to your existing account.

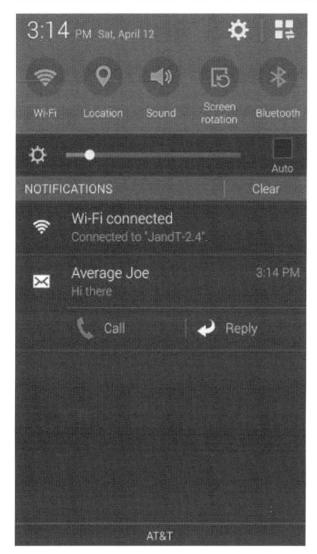

Figure 1: Notifications Screen

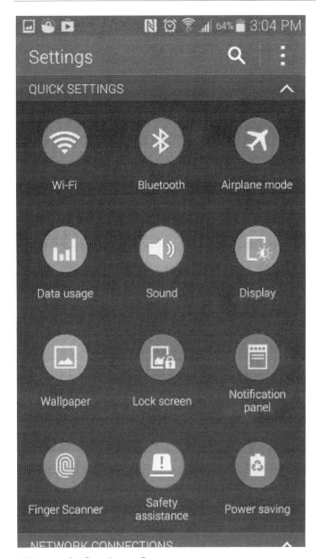

Figure 2: Settings Screen

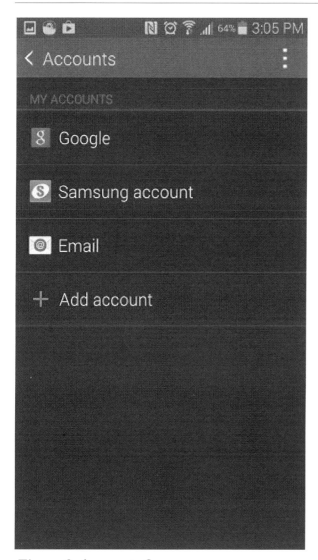

Figure 3: Accounts Screen

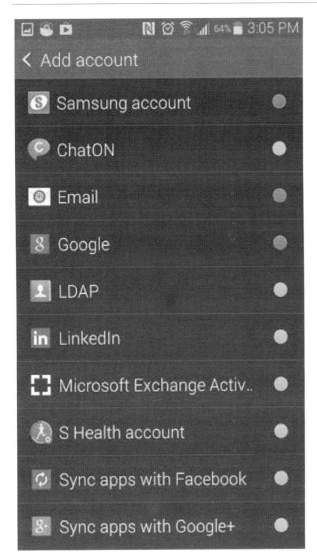

Figure 4: Add Account Screen

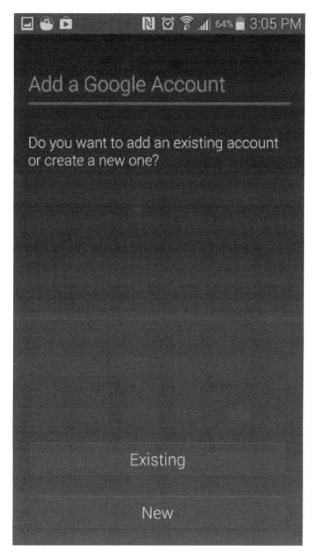

Figure 5: Add Google Account Screen

2. Reading Email (Gmail App)

You can read your email on the Galaxy S5 using the Gmail application. To read email:

1. Touch the ![icon] icon on the Home screen, or touch the ![icon] icon and then touch the ![icon] icon. The Gmail application opens and the Inbox appears, as shown in **Figure 6**.
2. Touch an email in the list. The email opens.
3. Touch the screen and move your finger to the left or right to view the previous or next email, respectively. The email appears.

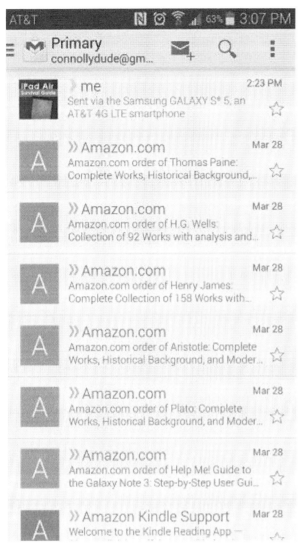

Figure 6: Gmail Inbox

3. Sending an Email (Gmail App)

Compose email directly from the Galaxy S5 using the Gmail application. To write an email while using the Gmail application:

1. Open the Inbox. Refer to *"Reading Email (Gmail App)"* on page 189 to learn how.
2. Touch the ✉ icon at the top of the screen. The Compose screen appears, as shown in **Figure 7**.
3. Start typing the name of a contact for whom you have a saved email address. A list of suggestions appears.

4. Touch the contact's name. The contact's email address is inserted. Alternatively, you may type an email from scratch in the 'To' field.

5. Touch **Subject** and enter an optional topic for the email. Touch **Compose email** and enter a message. The subject and message are entered.

6. Touch the ⟋ button in the upper right-hand corner of the screen. The email is sent.

Figure 7: Compose Screen

4. Replying to and Forwarding Emails (Gmail App)

After receiving an email, you can reply to the sender or forward the email to a new recipient. To reply to, or forward, an email while using the Gmail application:

1. Open the Inbox. Refer to *"Reading Email (Gmail App)"* on page 189 to learn how.
2. Touch an email. The email opens.
3. Touch the ↰ icon next to the sender's email address, as outlined in **Figure 8**. A new email is generated with the sender's email address already entered in the 'To' field.
4. Enter a message and touch the ➤ button. The reply is sent.
5. Alternatively, touch the ⋮ icon to the right of the ↰ icon in step 3, and then touch **Reply all** or **Forward**. Choosing 'Reply all' will send a reply to all recipients of the original email. Choosing 'Forward' will send a copy of the message to a different recipient, requiring you to enter an email address in the 'To' field. Follow step 4 to reply to all recipients or to forward the email.

Figure 8: Reply Icon Outlined

5. Deleting Emails and Restoring Deleted Emails to the Inbox (Gmail App)

Deleting an email sends it to the Trash folder. To completely delete an email, the Trash folder must be emptied. To delete emails while using the Gmail application:

Warning: Emails in the Trash folder are permanently deleted after 30 days. Make sure that you retrieve the message before 30 days if you still need it.

1. Open the Inbox. Refer to "*Reading Email (Gmail App)*" on page 189 to learn how.
2. Touch the letter or picture to the left of the emails that you wish to delete, as shown in **Figure 9**. The letter will always be the first letter of the name or service involved in the

   email conversation. For instance, if it is an email conversation with George, touch the ⬚ icon. A picture will appear next to an email if the contact is associated with your Google+ account. The email conversation is selected and highlighted in blue.

3. Touch the ⬚ icon at the top of the screen, as outlined in **Figure 10**. The selected emails are deleted.

*Note: To clean up the Inbox without deleting emails, try archiving them. Archiving an email removes it from the Inbox and places it in the 'All Mail' folder. To archive an email, touch the email in the Inbox and slide your finger to the left or right. 'Archived' appears in place of the email in the Inbox. Touch **undo** to return the email to the Inbox.*

To restore deleted emails to the Inbox:

1. Open the Inbox. Refer to "*Reading Email (Email App)*" on page 174 to learn how.
2. Touch **Primary** in the upper left-hand corner of the screen. A list of email folders appears, as shown in **Figure 11**.
3. Scroll down and touch **Trash**. The Trash folder appears.
4. Touch the letter or picture to the left of the email that you wish to restore to the Inbox. The selected emails are highlighted.
5. Touch the ⬚ icon in the upper right-hand corner of the screen. The Move To options appear, as shown in **Figure 12**.
6. Touch **Primary**. The selected emails are moved to the Primary Inbox.

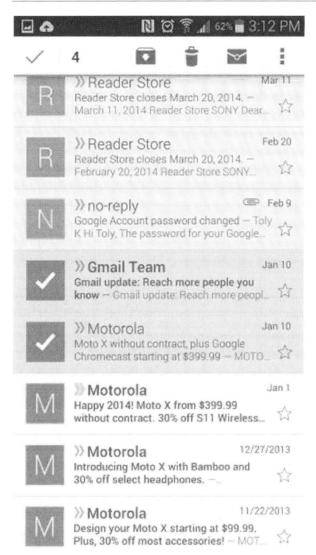

Figure 9: Selected Emails

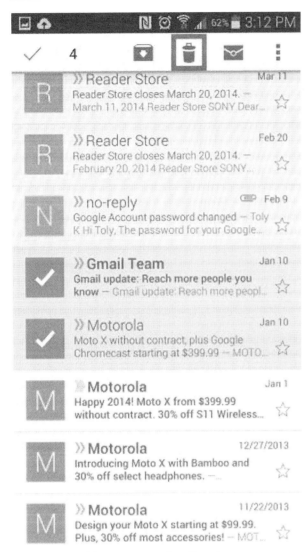

Figure 10: Trash Icon Outlined

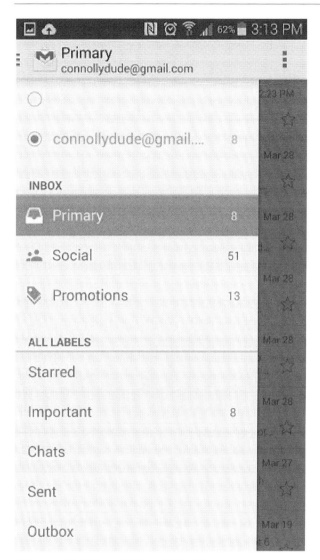

Figure 11: List of Email Folders

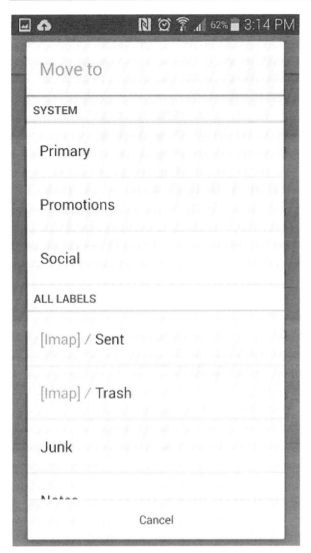

Figure 12: Move To Options

6. Adding Labels to Emails

Emails can be classified according to the nature of the message, such as 'work' or 'personal'. To add labels to emails while using the Gmail application:

1. Open the Inbox. Refer to *"Reading Email (Gmail App)" on page 189* to learn how.
2. Touch the letter or picture to the left of the email that you wish to label. The selected emails are highlighted.

3. Touch the ⋮ icon in the upper right-hand corner of the screen. The Inbox options appear, as shown in **Figure 13**.
4. Touch **Change labels**. A list of Gmail labels appears, as shown in **Figure 14**.
5. Touch as many labels as you wish. Touch **OK**. The labels are applied to the selected emails.

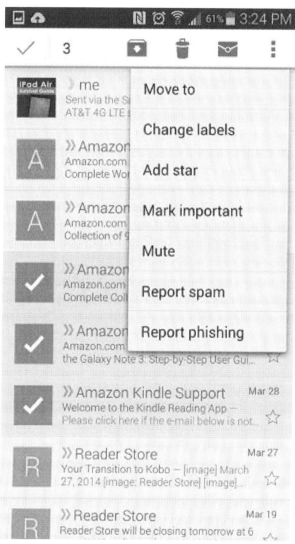

Figure 13: Inbox Options

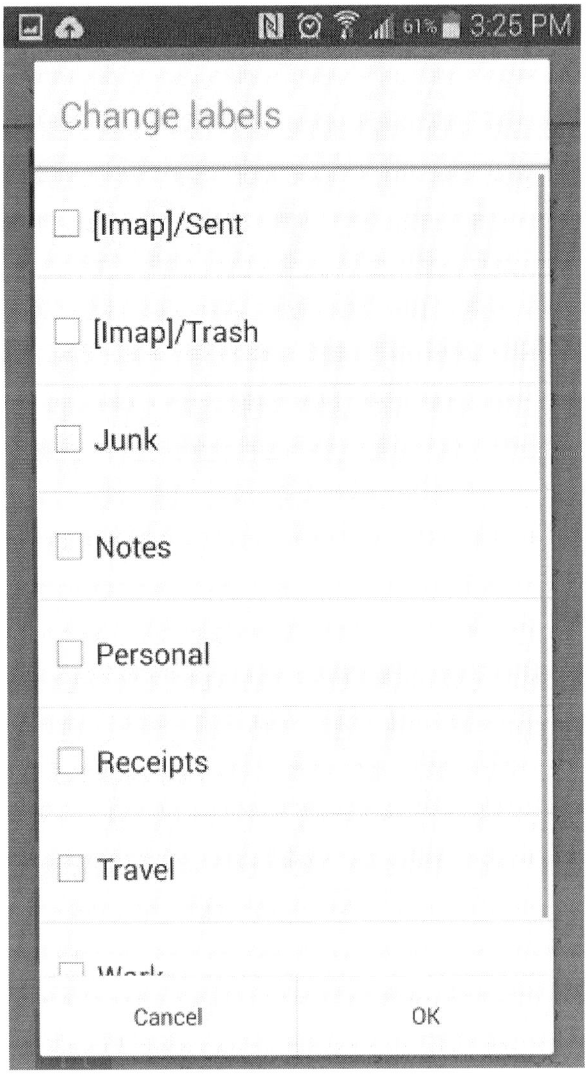

Figure 14: List of Gmail Labels

7. Searching the Inbox (Gmail App)

To find an email in the Inbox, use the search function, which searches email addresses, message content, and subject lines. To search the Inbox while using the Gmail application:

1. Open the Inbox. Refer to *"Reading Email (Gmail App)" on page 189* to learn how.

2. Touch the 🔍 icon in the upper right-hand corner of the screen. The virtual keyboard appears.

3. Enter a search word or phrase, and touch the 🔍 button. The Galaxy S5 searches the Inbox, and a list of matching results appears.

8. Ignoring New Messages in a Conversation

If you are included in an email conversation between multiple people that no longer pertains to you, you can set Gmail to prevent all emails in that conversation from reaching your Inbox. This action is called 'Muting' a conversation. To mute a conversation:

Note: Any new emails in the conversation that are addressed only to you will still appear in your inbox.

1. Open the Inbox. Refer to *"Reading Email (Gmail App)" on page 189* to learn how.
2. Touch the letter or picture to the left of the email that you wish to mute. The selected emails are highlighted.
3. Touch the ⋮ icon in the upper right-hand corner of the screen. The Inbox options appear.
4. Touch **Mute**. The conversations are muted, and only emails addressed solely to you will appear.

9. Blocking All Emails from a Specific Sender

If you receive unwanted emails from the same email address, such as a solicitor of unwanted products or services, you may block the sender altogether by marking the email as 'Spam'. To block emails from a specific sender:

1. Open the Inbox. Refer to *"Reading Email (Gmail App)" on page 189* to learn how.
2. Touch the letter or picture to the left of the email whose sender you wish to block. The selected emails are highlighted.
3. Touch the ⋮ icon in the upper right-hand corner of the screen. The Inbox options appear.
4. Touch **Report spam**. The selected emails, and all future emails from the selected senders, will be moved directly to the Spam folder.

10. Adjusting the General Gmail Preferences

You may customize the Gmail application by adjusting its settings. To adjust the general Gmail preferences while using the Gmail application:

1. Touch and hold the ⬛ key while using the Gmail application. The Gmail menu appears.
2. Touch **Settings**. The Gmail Settings screen appears, as shown in **Figure 15**.
3. Touch **General settings**. The General Settings screen appears, as shown in **Figure 16**.
4. Touch one of the following options to adjust the corresponding setting:

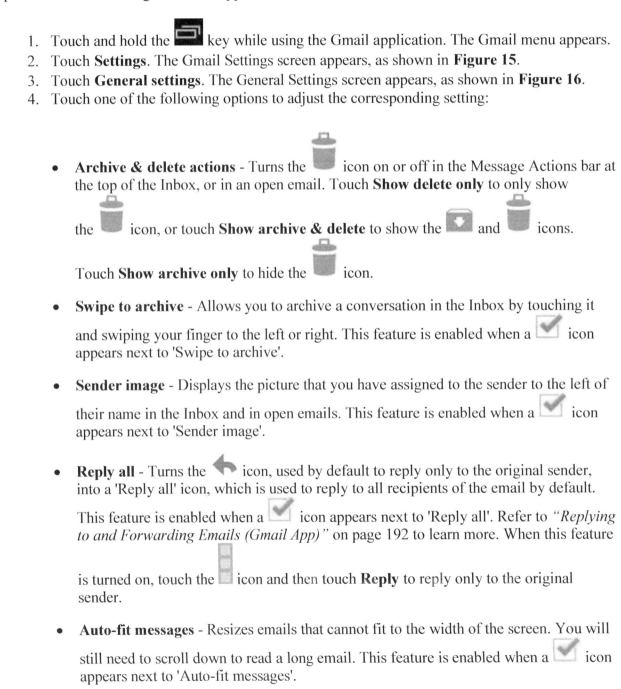

- **Archive & delete actions** - Turns the 🗑 icon on or off in the Message Actions bar at the top of the Inbox, or in an open email. Touch **Show delete only** to only show the 🗑 icon, or touch **Show archive & delete** to show the and 🗑 icons.

  Touch **Show archive only** to hide the 🗑 icon.

- **Swipe to archive** - Allows you to archive a conversation in the Inbox by touching it and swiping your finger to the left or right. This feature is enabled when a ✔ icon appears next to 'Swipe to archive'.

- **Sender image** - Displays the picture that you have assigned to the sender to the left of their name in the Inbox and in open emails. This feature is enabled when a ✔ icon appears next to 'Sender image'.

- **Reply all** - Turns the ↩ icon, used by default to reply only to the original sender, into a 'Reply all' icon, which is used to reply to all recipients of the email by default. This feature is enabled when a ✔ icon appears next to 'Reply all'. Refer to *"Replying to and Forwarding Emails (Gmail App)"* on page 192 to learn more. When this feature is turned on, touch the icon and then touch **Reply** to reply only to the original sender.

- **Auto-fit messages** - Resizes emails that cannot fit to the width of the screen. You will still need to scroll down to read a long email. This feature is enabled when a ✔ icon appears next to 'Auto-fit messages'.

- **Auto-advance** - Selects the screen that is displayed after deleting or archiving an open email. Touch **Auto-advance** and then touch **Newer**, **Older**, or **Conversation list** to select the next screen that will be displayed.

- **Message Actions** - Pins the message actions to a bar at the top of the screen when scrolling through an email. Touch **Message Actions** and then touch **Always show**, **Only show in portrait**, or **Don't show** to select when the message actions should remain pinned at the top of the screen.

- **Confirm before deleting** - Displays a confirmation dialog before deleting an email.

  This feature is enabled when a ☑ icon appears next to 'Confirm before deleting'. Refer to *"Deleting Emails and Restoring Deleted Emails to the Inbox (Gmail App)"* on page 194 to learn how to delete an email.

- **Confirm before archiving** - Displays a confirmation dialog before archiving an email.

  This feature is enabled when a ☑ icon appears next to 'Confirm before archiving'.

- **Confirm before sending** - Displays a confirmation dialog before sending an email.

  This feature is enabled when a ☑ icon appears next to 'Confirm before sending'. Refer to *"Sending an Email (Gmail App)"* on page 190 to learn more about sending email.

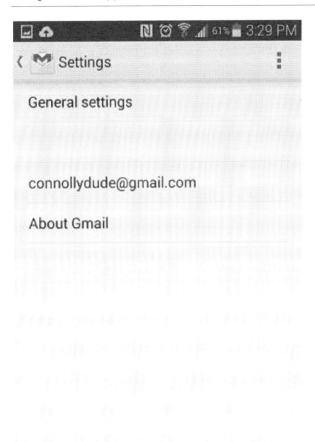

Figure 15: Gmail Settings Screen

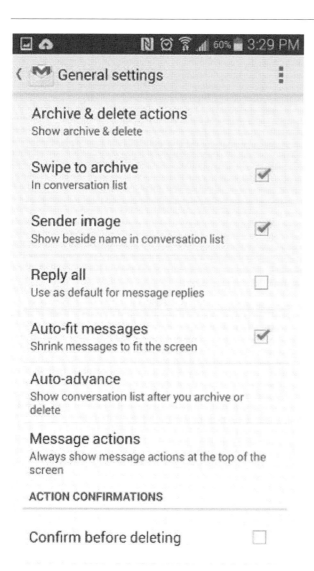

Figure 16: General Preferences Screen

11. Adjusting Gmail Account Preferences

You may adjust the settings particular to your Gmail account. To adjust Gmail account preferences:

1. Touch the ▣ key while using the Gmail application. The Gmail menu appears.
2. Touch **Settings**. The Gmail Settings screen appears.
3. Touch your email address. The Account Preferences screen appears, as shown in **Figure 17**.
4. Touch one of the following options to adjust the corresponding setting:

   - **Notifications** - Displays the M icon in the status bar when a new email arrives. This feature is enabled when a ✓ icon appears next to 'Notifications'.

   - **Inbox sound & vibrate** - Allows you to customize the notification method for newly received emails. Touch **Sound** or **Vibrate** on the following screen to select the sound your phone will make when a new email arrives, and whether the phone will vibrate.

   - **Signature** - Allows you to customize the signature that is attached to the end of every email that you send using your Galaxy S 5. Enter a signature and touch **OK** to set it.

   - **Vacation Responder** - Allows you to set an automatic email responder that will send the message that you type in the 'Message' field as a reply to every incoming email. Enter the start and end dates and touch the OFF switch to turn on the Vacation Responder.

Note: The Data Usage settings on the Account Preferences screen are for advanced users only. It is not necessary to adjust these settings.

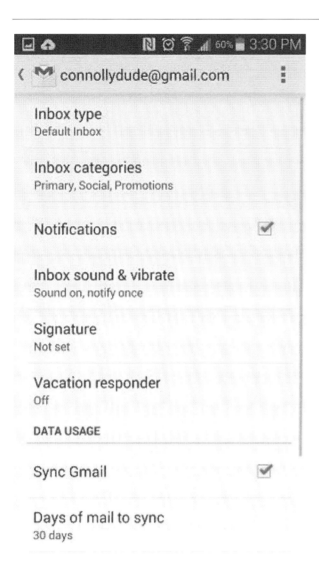

Figure 17: Account Preferences Screen

Managing Applications

Table of Contents

1. Setting Up a Google Account
2. Searching for an Application
3. Buying an Application
4. Uninstalling an Application
5. Adding an Application to Your Wishlist
6. Hiding Applications on the Application Screen
7. Closing Applications Running in the Background
8. Organizing Application Icons into Folders
9. Installing a Previously Purchased Application
10. Updating Installed Applications
11. Switching Between Google Accounts

1. Setting Up a Google Account

In order to buy applications, you will need to assign a Google account to the Galaxy S5. Refer to *"Adding a Google Account to the Phone"* on page 184 to learn how.

2. Searching for an Application

You can search for applications in the Play Store. There are two ways to search for applications:

Manual Search

To manually search for an application:

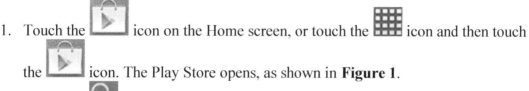

1. Touch the icon on the Home screen, or touch the icon and then touch the icon. The Play Store opens, as shown in **Figure 1**.
2. Touch the icon in the upper right-hand corner of the screen. The virtual keyboard appears.
3. Enter the name of an application or developer and touch the button in the bottom right-hand corner of the keyboard. The matching results appear grouped by media type, as shown in **Figure 2**.
4. Touch **APPS**. A list of matching application results appears, as shown in **Figure 3**.
5. Touch the name of an application. A description of the application appears.

Browse by Category

To browse applications by category:

1. Touch the icon on the Home screen, or touch the icon and then touch the icon. The Play Store opens.
2. Touch **Apps** or **Games**. A list of featured applications appears, as shown in **Figure 4**.
3. Touch the screen and move your finger to the left or right to browse the most popular paid or free applications. Keep swiping your finger to the right to select the Categories tab, where you can browse the application categories.
4. Touch the name of an application. A description of the application appears.

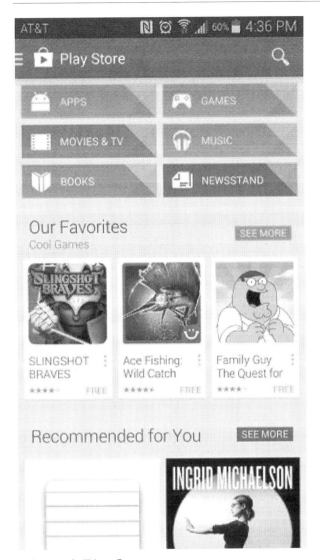

Figure 1: Play Store

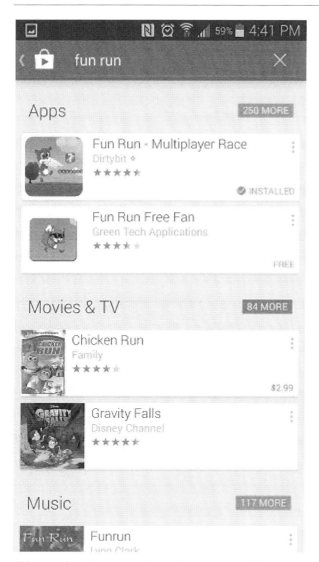

Figure 2: Matching Results Grouped by Media Type

Managing Applications

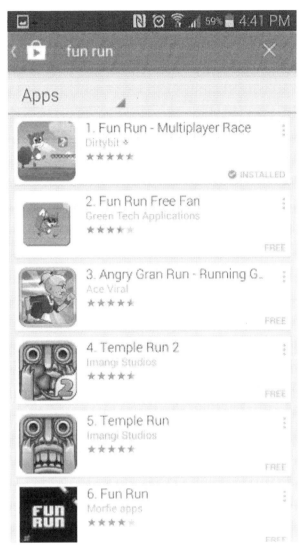

Figure 3: Matching Application Results

212

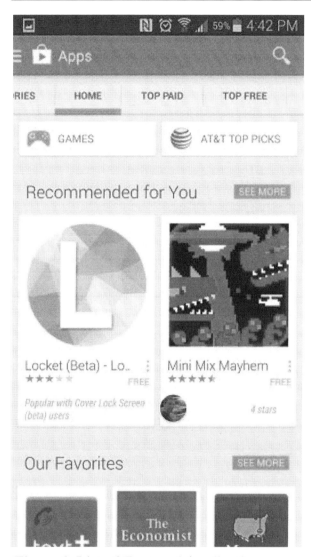

Figure 4: List of Featured Applications

3. Buying an Application

Applications can be purchased directly from the Galaxy S5 using the Play Store. To purchase an application from the Play Store:

1. Find an application. Refer to *"Searching for an Application"* on page 209 to learn more.
2. Touch the name of an application. The Application description appears, as shown in **Figure 5**.
3. Follow the instructions below to download the application:

Installing Free Applications

Touch the INSTALL button. The Permissions screen appears, as shown in **Figure 6**. Touch the ACCEPT button. The application begins to download, and the progress is shown. Touch **OPEN** to run the application when it is finished downloading and installing.

Installing Paid Applications

Touch the price of the application. The Permissions screen appears. Touch the ACCEPT button. The application begins to download and the progress is shown. You may also need to enter your Google password before the application can be purchased. Touch **OPEN** to run the application when it is finished downloading and installing.

Note: When purchasing an application for the first time, Google Checkout asks for your credit card information. The information is saved and used for all subsequent purchases.

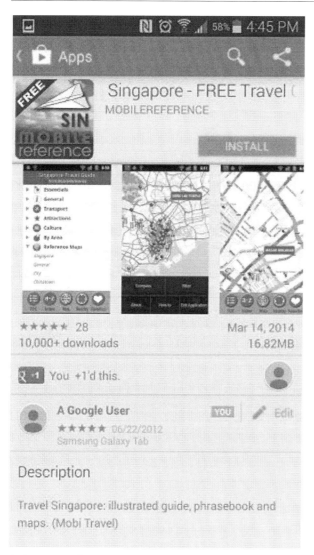

Figure 5: Application Description

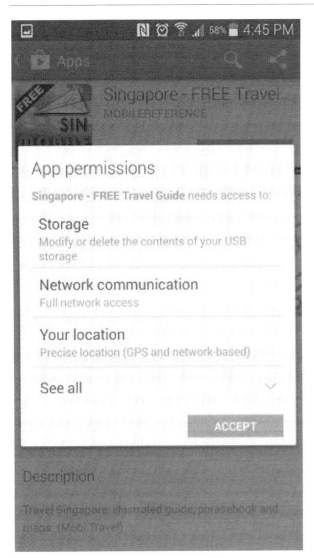

Figure 6: Permissions Screen

4. Uninstalling an Application

Within the first 15 minutes of purchasing an application, it can be uninstalled for a full refund. After 15 minutes have passed, the following instructions only apply to uninstalling an application without receiving a refund. To request a refund and uninstall an application while using the Play Store:

1. Touch the left side of the screen and slide your finger to the right. The Play Store menu appears, as shown in **Figure 7**.
2. Touch **My Apps**. The My Apps screen appears, as shown in **Figure 8**.
3. Touch the application that you wish to remove. The Application description appears.

4. Touch **REFUND** if less than 15 minutes have passed. Otherwise, touch **UNINSTALL**. The application is uninstalled and a refund is given if less than 15 minutes have passed.

*Note: If uninstalling without a refund, a confirmation dialog appears after touching Uninstall. Touch **OK**. The application is uninstalled. You can always re-download an application that was purchased and uninstalled for free. Refer to "Installing a Previously Purchased Application" on page 226 to learn how to re-download an application.*

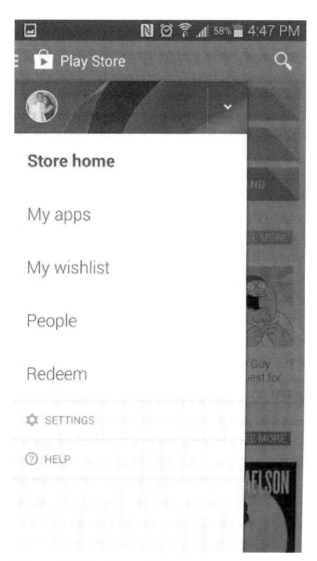

Figure 7: Play Store Menu

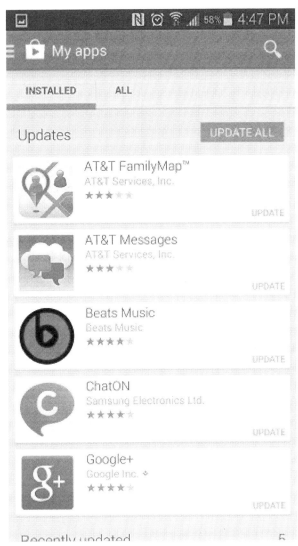

Figure 8: My Apps Screen

5. Adding an Application to Your Wishlist

You may find an application that you like but do not wish to purchase it right away. If you wish to save an application as a favorite, you may add it to your Wishlist. To add an application to your Wishlist:

1. Find an application. Refer to **Searching for an Application** to learn more.
2. Touch the name of an application. The Application Description screen appears.

3. Touch the ▢ icon at the top of the screen. The application is added to your Wishlist.

4. Touch the left side of the screen and slide your finger to the right, and then touch **My wishlist** while using the Play Store. The Wishlist appears, as shown in **Figure 9**.

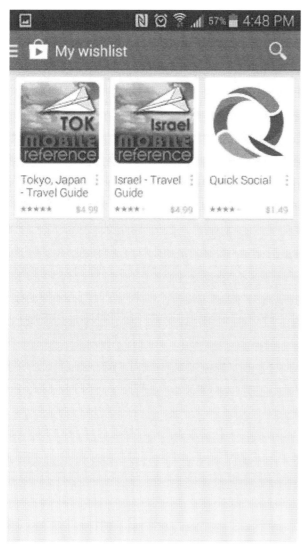

Figure 9: Wishlist

6. Hiding Applications on the Application Screen

You may wish to prevent other people that use your phone, such as your children, from using certain applications. To hide applications:

1. Touch the ⊞ icon in the lower right-hand corner of the Home screen. The Application screen appears.

2. Touch and hold the ⊡ key. The Application Screen menu appears, as shown in **Figure 10**.

3. Touch **Hide applications**. Applications may now be selected.

4. Touch each application that you wish to hide. A ✓ mark appears next to each selected application, as shown in **Figure 11**.

5. Touch **Done** in the upper right-hand corner of the screen. The selected applications are hidden. To show hidden applications, follow steps 1-3 in this section, touching **Show hidden applications** in step 3.

Note: If an application has already been added to a Home screen, it will not be automatically hidden on that Home screen. Refer to "Organizing Home Screen Objects" *on page 17 to learn how to remove an application icon from the Home screen.*

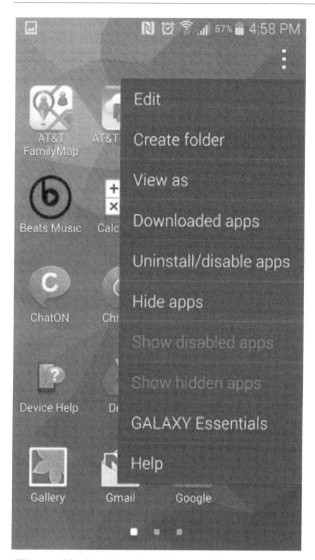

Figure 10: Application Screen Menu

Figure 11: Selected Applications

7. Closing Applications Running in the Background

Most applications will keep running even after they are exited, and some take up a considerable amount of memory. To speed up the performance of the Galaxy S5, try closing some or all of these applications while they are not in use. To close an application running in the background, press

the ⬚ key. A list of running applications appears, as shown in **Figure 12**. Touch an application and slide your finger to the left or right, if viewing the screen in Portrait mode, or slide your finger up or down if viewing the screen in Landscape mode. The application is closed and disappears from the list.

Figure 12: List of Running Applications

8. Organizing Application Icons into Folders

The Galaxy S5 can store applications in folders on the Home screens. This is especially useful to reduce clutter and find applications faster. To create a folder on the Home screen:

1. Touch and hold an application icon. The phone briefly vibrates and 'Create folder' appears at the top of the screen, as outlined in **Figure 13**.
2. Drag the application icon on top of 'Create folder' and release the screen. The Create Folder dialog appears.

3. Enter a name for the folder and touch **OK**. The folder is created, as outlined in red in **Figure 14**.

4. Touch the new folder. The folder opens and the contained applications appear, as shown in **Figure 15**.

5. Touch and hold an icon inside a folder and drag it anywhere outside of the folder. The application icon is removed from the folder.

6. Touch and hold any icon that is not in a folder and drag it on top of the new folder. The icon is added to the folder.

Figure 13: Creating a Folder

Figure 14: Folder Created

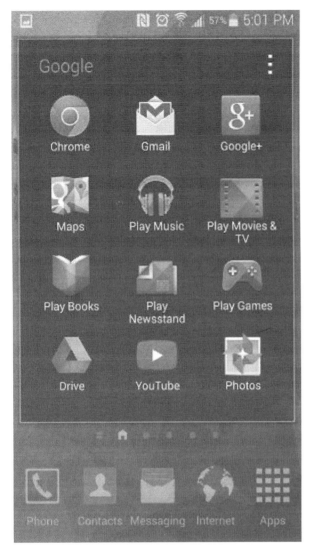

Figure 15: Applications in a Folder

9. Installing a Previously Purchased Application

After purchasing an application on an Android device registered to your account, you can download the same application for free on any Android device registered to the same account. To install previously purchased applications while using the Play Store:

1. Touch the left side of the screen and slide your finger to the right. The Play Store menu appears.
2. Touch **My Apps**. The My Apps screen appears.

3. Touch the screen and move your finger to the right. A list of all applications, both installed and uninstalled, appears.
4. Touch the name of an application. The Application description appears. If you cannot find the application, refer to *"Switching between Google Accounts"* on page 227 to learn how to view applications purchased under a different Google account registered to your phone.
5. Touch the INSTALL button. The Permissions screen appears.
6. Touch the ACCEPT button. The application is installed on your phone.

10. Updating Installed Applications

Application developers will sometimes release updates for their applications. To update your installed applications while using the Play Store:

1. Touch the left side of the screen and slide your finger to the right. The Play Store menu appears.
2. Touch **My Apps**. The My Apps screen appears.
3. Touch an application under 'Updates'. The Application description appears. If there are no applications under 'Updates', then there are no updates available for your installed applications.
4. Touch **UPDATE**. The Permissions screen appears.
5. Touch the ACCEPT button. The application is updated.

*Note: You can also touch **UPDATE ALL** to the right of 'Updates' to update all of your out-of-date applications at once. There is no confirmation dialog when using this method.*

11. Switching between Google Accounts

If you use more than one Google account on your phone, you may wish to switch to another account to download and manage applications. To switch between Google Accounts while using the Play Store:

1. Touch the left side of the screen and slide your finger to the right. The Play Store menu appears.

   Touch the ☑ icon next to your email address. A list of registered Google accounts appears, as shown in **Figure 16**. If you do not see the Google account, you may need to add it to your phone. Refer to *"Adding a Google Account to the Phone"* on page 184 to learn how.

2. Touch an account. The selected account will now be used to purchase and manage applications.

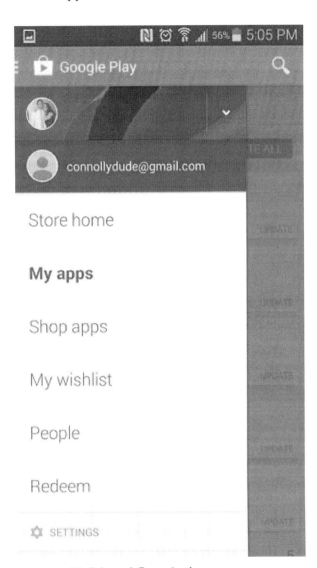

Figure 16: List of Google Accounts

Using the S Voice Assistant

S Voice is a voice-activated assistant that comes with the Galaxy S5. Follow the tips in this chapter to use S Voice to its full potential. In each of the sections, the text between the < arrows > signifies where you should fill in what you need. For instance, "Call <contact name>" could become "Call Suzie."

Table of Contents

1. Calling, Sending Messages, and Taking Notes
2. Searching the Web for General Information
3. Finding Information about Music and Movies
4. Navigating to a Webpage
5. Finding Locations and Attractions
6. Looking Up Times and Dates
7. Asking about the Weather

1. Calling, Sending Messages, and Taking Notes

To make a call or send a message using the S Voice assistant, press the **Home** button twice quickly to speak. Say one of the following phrases:

- Call <contact name>
- Text <contact name> <message>
- Note to self <note>
- Remind me to <task> at <time>
- Set alarm for <time>

Note: These phrases are only suggestions. S Voice is flexible, and you can use many synonymous phrases.

2. Searching the Web for General Information

To search the web using the S Voice assistant, press the **Home** button twice quickly to speak. Say one of the following phrases:

- When was <name> born?
- What is <object>?
- Define <word>
- Show pictures of <item>
- Stock <company>
- Who is the CEO of <company>?

Note: These phrases are only suggestions. S Voice is flexible, and you can use many synonymous phrases.

3. Finding Information about Music and Movies

To find entertainment information on the web or your phone using the S Voice assistant, press the **Home** button twice quickly to speak. Say one of the following phrases:

- Tell me show times for the <movie>
- Play <name of song> or <name of artist>\
- Who directed <movie name>?
- What movie was <actor/actress name> in?
- When was <movie name> released?

Note: These phrases are only suggestions. S Voice is flexible, and you can use many synonymous phrases.

4. Navigating to a Webpage

To navigate to a webpage using the S Voice assistant, press the **Home** button twice quickly to speak. Say one of the following phrases:

- Browse to <website>
- Open <website>

Note: These phrases are only suggestions. S Voice is flexible, and you can use many synonymous phrases.

5. Finding Locations and Attractions

To find information regarding certain locations using the S Voice assistant, press the **Home** button twice quickly to speak. Say one of the following phrases:

- Where is the closest <store name>?
- Directions to <place name>
- Navigate to <place name>
- Nearest <place>
- What time is it in <city/state/country>?
- What is the date in <city/state/country>?
- What language is spoken in <country/region>?
- What is the currency of <country>?
- What is the National Anthem of <country>?
- What is the capital of <country/state>?
- What is the state bird of <state>?
- What is the population of <city/state/country>?
- What does <country>'s flag look like?

Note: These phrases are only suggestions. S Voice is flexible, and you can use many synonymous phrases.

6. Looking Up Times and Dates

To look up times and dates using the S Voice assistant, press the **Home** button twice quickly to speak. Say one of the following phrases:

- When is daylight savings?
- When does <season> start?
- When is <sundown>?
- When is <sunrise>?
- When is <holiday>?
- What time zone is <state/country> in?

Note: These phrases are only suggestions. S Voice is flexible, and you can use many synonymous phrases.

7. Asking about the Weather

To find out about the weather using the S Voice assistant, press the **Home** button twice quickly to speak. Say one of the following phrases:

- What is the weather <today/ tomorrow/ specific day>?
- What is the weather <today/ tomorrow/ specific day> in <location>?
- Do I need an umbrella <today/ tomorrow/ specific day>?
- Do I need an umbrella <today/ tomorrow/ specific day>in <location>?
- Do I need a jacket <today/ tomorrow/ specific day>?
- Do I need a jacket <today/ tomorrow/ specific day>in <location>?

Note: These phrases are only suggestions. S Voice is flexible, and you can use many synonymous phrases.

Adjusting the Wireless Settings

Table of Contents

1. Setting Up Wi-Fi
2. Setting Up Bluetooth
3. Turning Airplane Mode On or Off
4. Enabling or Disabling the Mobile Network
5. Turning Data Roaming On or Off
6. Turning Near Field Communication On or Off

1. Setting Up Wi-Fi

Use a nearby Wi-Fi hotspot or a home router to attain a much faster internet connection than 4G. Wi-Fi is required to download large applications. To turn on Wi-Fi:

1. Touch the top of the screen and slide your finger down. The Notifications appear, as shown in **Figure 1**.
2. Touch the icon in the upper right-hand corner of the screen. The Settings screen appears, as shown in **Figure 2**.
3. Touch the icon. The Wi-Fi settings screen appears.
4. Touch the switch in the upper right-hand corner of the screen. The switch appears and Wi-Fi is turned on. A list of available Wi-Fi networks appears, as shown in **Figure 3**.
5. Touch a Wi-Fi network. The Wi-Fi Network Password prompt appears, if the network is password-protected. Otherwise, the Galaxy S5 connects to the Wi-Fi network.
6. Enter the network password, if required, which is usually found on your wireless router. Touch **Connect**. The Galaxy S5 connects to the Wi-Fi network.

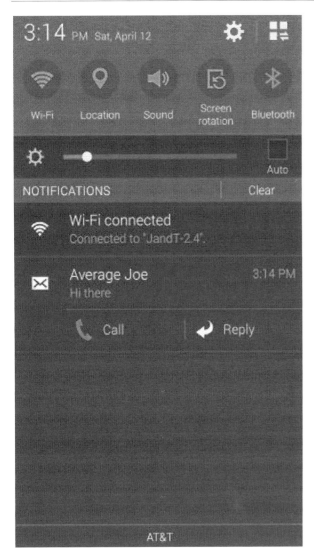

Figure 1: Application Screen

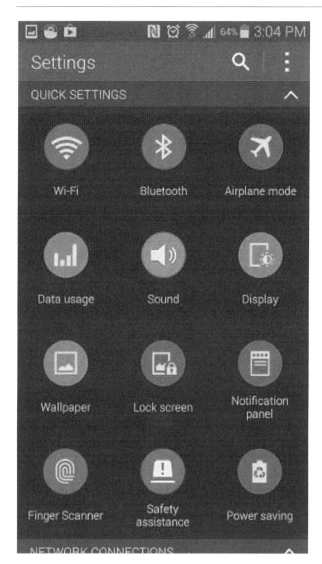

Figure 2: Settings Screen

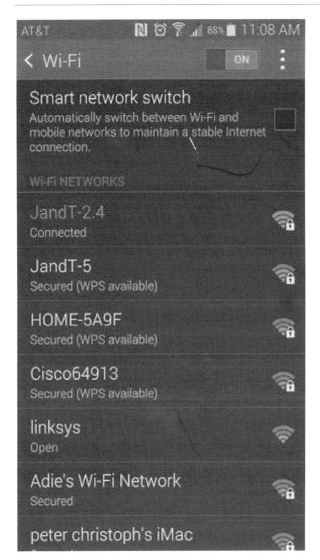

Figure 3: List of Available Wi-Fi Networks

2. Setting Up Bluetooth

To use a wireless Bluetooth headset, you will need to turn on Bluetooth. However, if you leave it on while your headset is not in use, it will significantly reduce the battery life of your phone. To turn Bluetooth on or off:

1. Touch the top of the screen and slide your finger down. The Notifications appear.

2. Touch the ⚙ icon in the upper right-hand corner of the screen. The Settings screen appears.

3. Touch the ✳ icon. The Bluetooth Settings screen appears.

4. Touch the OFF switch in the upper right-hand corner of the screen. The ON switch appears and Bluetooth is turned on. A list of Bluetooth devices that are within range and able to pair with the Galaxy S5 appears, as shown in **Figure 4**. To make the Galaxy S5 visible to other devices, touch **SAMSUNG-SM-G900A** at the top of the Bluetooth Settings screen. The Galaxy S5 becomes visible for two minutes.

5. Touch a device in the list. The Pairing Request window appears, as shown in **Figure 5**.

6. Touch **OK** (or **Pair**) on both devices. The devices are paired.

7. Touch the ON switch in the upper right-hand corner of the screen. Bluetooth is turned off and all paired devices are disconnected.

Figure 4: List of Available Bluetooth Devices

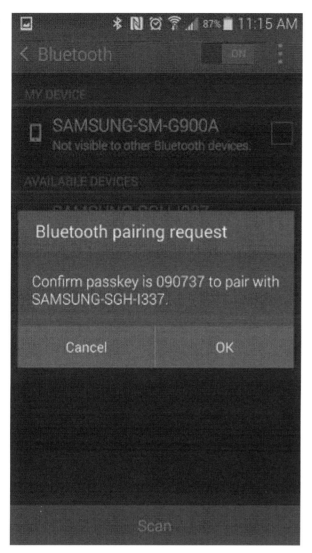

Figure 5: Pairing Request Window

3. Turning Airplane Mode On or Off

Airplanes do not allow wireless communications while in flight. Continue using your phone by enabling Airplane Mode before take-off. You may not place or receive calls, send or receive text messages or emails, or surf the Web while in Airplane Mode. Airplane Mode is also useful when traveling outside of your area of service to avoid any roaming charges, and to preserve battery life. To turn Airplane Mode on or off:

1. Press and hold the **Power** button. The Device Options menu appears, as shown in **Figure 6**.

2. Touch **Airplane mode**. A confirmation dialog appears.
3. Touch **OK**. Airplane mode is turned on.
4. Repeat steps 1-3 to turn Airplane mode off.

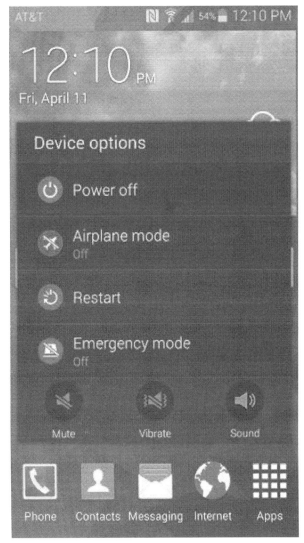

Figure 6: Device Options Menu

4. Enabling or Disabling the Mobile Network

Turning the mobile network on allows you to make calls, and allows the Galaxy S5 to use data for email and internet. Disabling the mobile network is useful when you are in an area with little or no service in order to conserve battery life. The mobile network is turned on by default. To enable or disable the mobile network:

1. Touch the top of the screen and slide your finger down. The Notifications appear.

2. Touch the ⚙ icon in the upper right-hand corner of the screen. The Settings screen appears.

3. Scroll down and touch the 📶 icon. The More Networks screen appears, as shown in **Figure 7**. If you do not see the 📶 icon, touch **Network Connections** to reveal the network settings.

4. Touch **Mobile networks**. The Mobile Network Settings screen appears, as shown in **Figure 8**.

5. Touch **Mobile data**. The ✓ mark next to 'Data enabled' disappears, and the mobile network is disabled.

6. Touch **Mobile data** again. The ✓ mark appears next to 'Data enabled', and the Mobile Network is enabled.

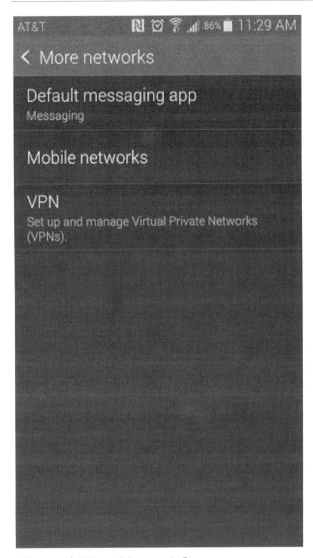

Figure 7: More Network Screen

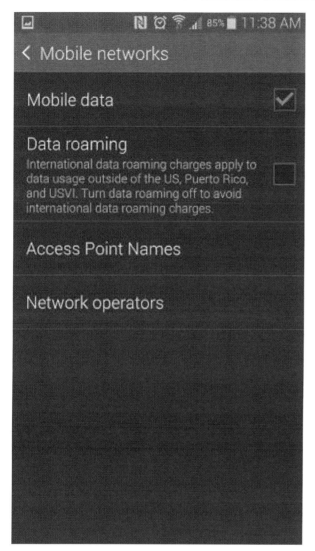

Figure 8: Mobile Network Settings Screen

5. Turning Data Roaming On or Off

When you are in an area with no wireless coverage, the Galaxy S5 can use the Data Roaming feature to acquire signal from other networks. Be aware that Data Roaming can be extremely costly. Contact your network provider for details. By default, Data Roaming is turned off. To turn Data Roaming on or off:

1. Touch the top of the screen and slide your finger down. The Notifications appear.

2. Touch the ⚙ icon in the upper right-hand corner of the screen. The Settings screen appears.

3. Scroll down and touch the ![icon] icon. The More Networks screen appears. If you do not see the ![icon] icon, touch **Network Connections** to reveal the network settings.

4. Touch **Mobile networks**. The Mobile Network Settings screen appears.

5. Touch **Data roaming**. The ✓ mark appears next to 'Data roaming', and the feature is turned on.

6. Touch **Data enabled**. The ✓ mark next to 'Data roaming' disappears, and the feature is turned off.

6. Turning Near Field Communication On or Off

The Galaxy S5 can use Near Field Communication (NFC) to "talk" to other devices in order to transmit data, such as pictures or videos. When sharing information, you may select **Android Beam** to transmit the information to another NFC-enabled phone. By default, NFC is turned on, and it uses a minimal amount of battery as long as it is not in use. If for any reason you wish to turn it off, you may do so. To turn NFC on or off:

1. Touch the top of the screen and slide your finger down. The Notifications appear.

2. Touch the ![icon] icon in the upper right-hand corner of the screen. The Settings screen appears.

3. Scroll down and touch the ![icon] icon. The NFC settings screen appears, as shown in **Figure 9**.

4. Touch the ![ON switch] switch at the top of the screen. The ![OFF switch] switch appears and NFC is turned off.

5. Touch the ![OFF switch] switch at the top of the screen. The ![ON switch] switch appears and NFC is turned on.

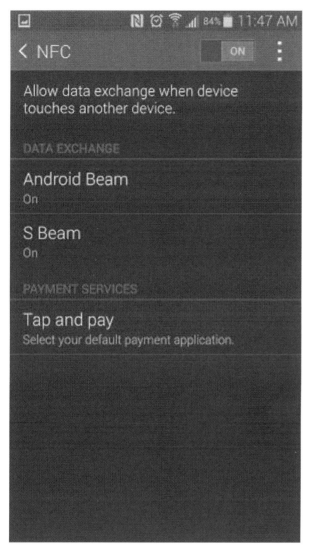

Figure 9: NFC Settings Screen

Adjusting the Sound Settings

Table of Contents

1. Setting the Vibration Intensity
2. Setting the Ringtone, Media, and Alarm Volume
3. Setting the Default Ringtone
4. Setting the Default Vibration Pattern
5. Setting the Default Notification Sound
6. Turning Ringer Vibration On or Off
7. Turning System Sounds On or Off

1. Setting the Vibration Intensity

The Galaxy S5 can vibrate during incoming calls, notifications, and when you touch either the ⬜ or ⬅ key. To set the intensity of the vibration:

1. Touch the top of the screen and slide your finger down. The Notifications appear, as shown in **Figure 1**.
2. Touch the ⚙ icon in the upper right-hand corner of the screen. The Settings screen appears, as shown in **Figure 2**.
3. Touch the 🔊 icon at the top of the screen. The Sound Settings screen appears, as shown in **Figure 3**.
4. Touch **Vibration intensity**. The Vibration Intensity window appears, as shown in **Figure 4**.
5. Touch the ◀○▶ below the corresponding vibration type and drag it to the left to decrease the volume or to the right to increase it. Release the screen. The vibration is adjusted, and the phone vibrates to preview the vibration intensity.
6. Touch **OK**. The vibration intensity is set.

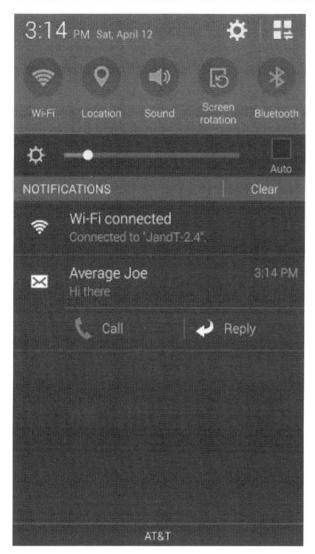

Figure 1: Notifications

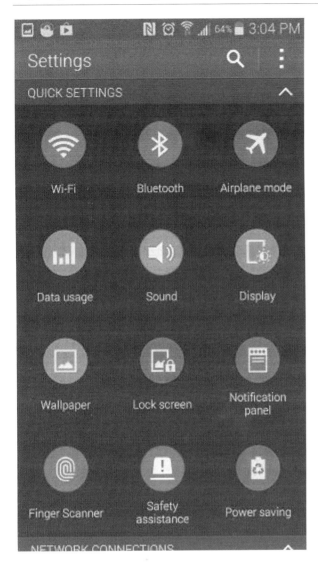

Figure 2: Settings Screen

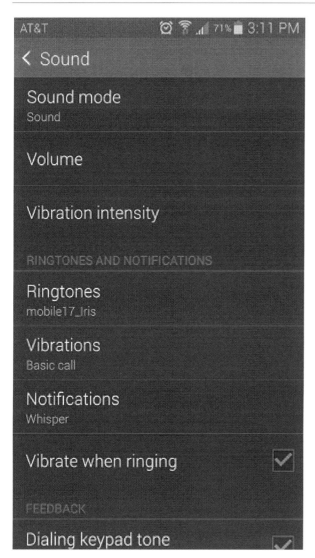

Figure 3: Sound Settings Screen

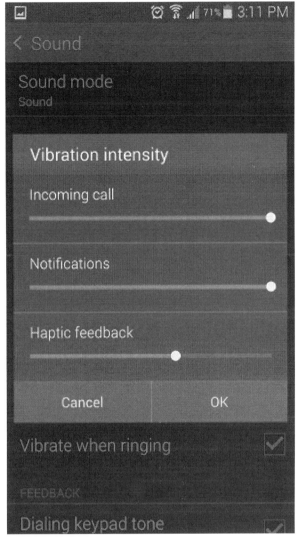

Figure 4: Vibration Intensity Window

2. Setting the Ringtone, Media, and Alarm Volume

The volume for various notifications can be set separately. To set the notification volumes:

1. Touch the top of the screen and slide your finger down. The Notifications appear.

2. Touch the ⚙ icon in the upper right-hand corner of the screen. The Settings screen appears.

3. Touch the 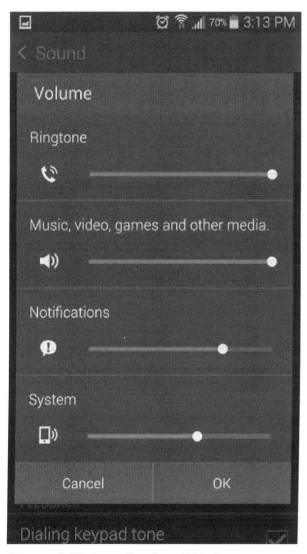 icon at the top of the screen. The Sound Settings screen appears.
4. Touch **Volume**. The Volume Settings window appears, as shown in **Figure 5**.
5. Touch the ◼◯◼ below the corresponding volume type, and drag it to the left to decrease the volume or to the right to increase it. Release the screen. The volume is adjusted, and a sound plays to preview the volume level.
6. Touch **OK**. The volume is set.

Note: The 'System' volume encompasses all system sounds, including the Alarm volume.

Figure 5: Volume Settings Window

3. Setting the Default Ringtone

You may change the ringtone that sounds every time somebody calls you. To set the default ringtone:

1. Touch the top of the screen and slide your finger down. The Notifications appear.

2. Touch the ⚙ icon in the upper right-hand corner of the screen. The Settings screen appears.

3. Touch the 🔊 icon at the top of the screen. The Sound Settings screen appears.

4. Touch **Ringtones**. A list of available ringtones appears, as shown in **Figure 6**. The ringtone that is currently in use has a ⦿ button next to it.

5. Touch a ringtone. A preview of the entire ringtone is played.

6. Touch **OK**. The default ringtone is set.

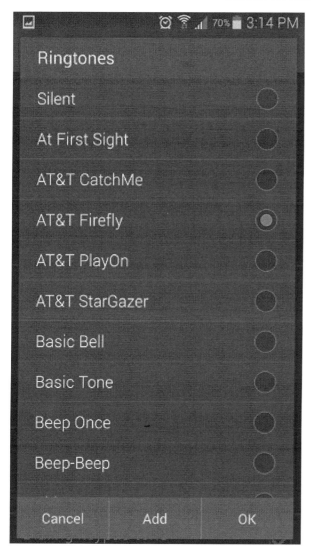

Figure 6: List of Available Ringtones

4. Setting the Default Vibration Pattern

The Galaxy S5 can use a series of vibrations, similar to Morse code, to create a custom pattern that allows you to determine the identity of a caller without looking at the phone. To set the default vibration pattern:

1. Touch the top of the screen and slide your finger down. The Notifications appear.

2. Touch the ⚙ icon in the upper right-hand corner of the screen. The Settings screen appears.

3. Touch the 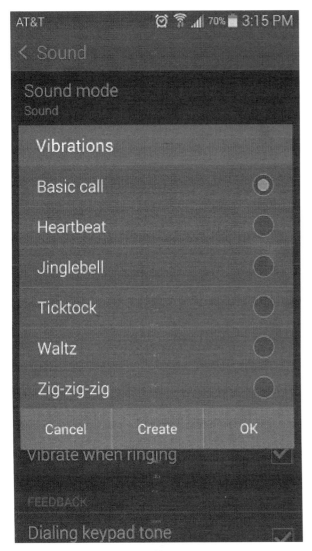 icon at the top of the screen. The Sound Settings screen appears.
4. Touch **Vibrations** under 'Ringtones and notifications'. A list of vibration patterns appears, as shown in **Figure 7**. The pattern that is currently in use has a ⬤ button next to it.
5. Touch a vibration pattern. The phone vibrates to preview the pattern.
6. Touch **OK**. The default vibration pattern is set.

Figure 7: List of Vibration Patterns

5. Setting the Default Notification Sound

When an event occurs, such as an incoming text or voicemail, a sound is played, known as the Notification sound. To change the default Notification sound:

1. Touch the top of the screen and slide your finger down. The Notifications appear.

2. Touch the ⚙ icon in the upper right-hand corner of the screen. The Settings screen appears.

3. Touch the 🔊 icon at the top of the screen. The Sound Settings screen appears.

4. Touch **Notifications**. A list of available notification sounds appears, as shown in **Figure 8**.

    The notification sound that is currently in use has a ⦿ button next to it.

5. Touch a notification sound. A preview of the sound is played.

6. Touch **OK**. The default notification sound is set.

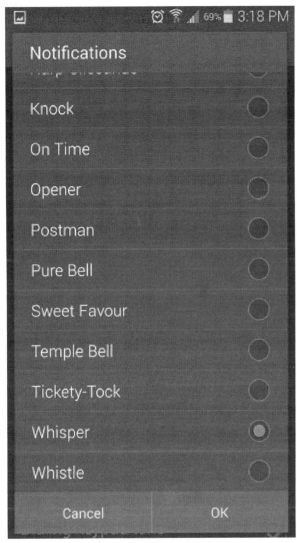

Figure 8: List of Available Notification Sounds

6. Turning Ringer Vibration On or Off

The Galaxy S5 can vibrate every time the ringtone sounds. Before you can adjust this setting, you must turn on the ringtone volume. You can do so by pressing the **Volume Up** button on the left side of the phone. To turn ringer vibration on or off:

1. Touch the top of the screen and slide your finger down. The Notifications appear.

2. Touch the ⚙ icon in the upper right-hand corner of the screen. The Settings screen appears.

3. Touch the ![sound icon] icon at the top of the screen. The Sound Settings screen appears.

4. Touch **Vibrate when ringing**. A ✓ mark appears next to 'Vibrate when ringing', and the feature is turned on.

5. Touch **Vibrate when ringing** again. The ✓ mark disappears, and the feature is turned off.

7. Turning System Sounds On or Off

Some system sounds, such as dial pad touch tones and screen lock sounds, can be turned on or off. To turn system sounds on or off:

1. Touch the top of the screen and slide your finger down. The Notifications appear.

2. Touch the ![settings icon] icon in the upper right-hand corner of the screen. The Settings screen appears.

3. Touch the ![sound icon] icon at the top of the screen. The Sound Settings screen appears.

4. Touch one of the following options under 'System' to turn the corresponding sound on or off:

   - **Dial keypad tone** - Turns the sounds made when touching a number on the dial pad on or off.
   - **Touch sounds** - Turns the sounds made when making a selection on the screen on or off.
   - **Screen lock sound** - Turns the sounds made when locking and unlocking the screen on or off.
   - **Haptic feedback** - Turns the vibration made when pressing the ![menu key] key or ![back key] key on or off.
   - **Sound when tapped (under Samsung Keyboard)** - Turns the sounds made when touching a key on the keyboard on or off.
   - **Vibrate when tapped (under Samsung Keyboard)** - Turns the vibrations made when touching keys on the keyboard on or off.

Adjusting the Display Settings

Table of Contents

1. Adjusting the Brightness
2. Changing the Wallpaper
3. Turning Multi Window On or Off
4. Turning Auto-Rotate On or Off
5. Setting the Screen Timeout
6. Changing the Font
7. Setting the Touch Key Light Duration
8. Turning the Battery Percentage On or Off
9. Turning High Touch Sensitivity On or Off
10. Setting the Home Screen Mode
11. Turning Motions and Gestures On or Off
12. Turning Air View On or Off
13. Customizing the LED Notification Light

1. Adjusting the Brightness

The Galaxy S5 can be set to automatically detect lighting conditions, and adjust the brightness of the screen accordingly. When Automatic Brightness is turned off, a single brightness setting is maintained in any lighting. To customize the brightness settings:

1. Touch the top of the screen and slide your finger down. The Notifications appear, as shown in **Figure 1**.

2. Touch the icon in the upper right-hand corner of the screen. The Settings screen appears, as shown in **Figure 2**.

3. Touch the icon at the top of the screen. The Display Settings screen appears, as shown in **Figure 3**.

4. Touch **Brightness**. The Brightness window appears. By default, Automatic Brightness is turned on.

5. Touch **Automatic brightness**. The mark next to 'Automatic brightness' disappears, and the feature is turned off. The Adjustment bar becomes active.

258

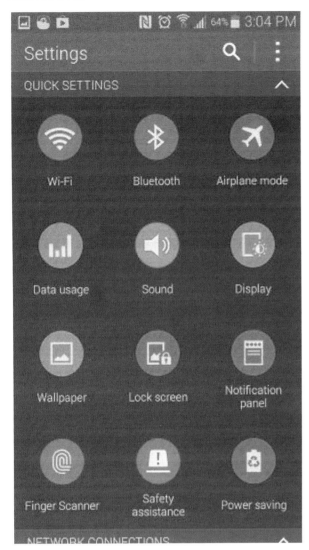

6. Touch and drag the slider to the left to decrease the brightness, or to the right to increase it. Touch **OK**. The brightness is adjusted. Alternatively, touch **Cancel** to continue using the Automatic Brightness feature.

Figure 1: Notifications

Figure 2: Settings Screen

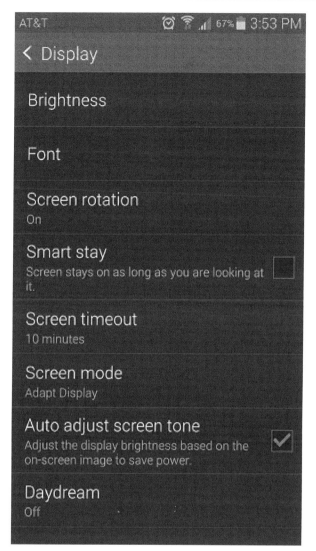

Figure 3: Display Settings Screen

2. Changing the Wallpaper

The wallpaper is the image that appears behind the application icons and widgets on the Home screens. To change the wallpaper:

1. Touch the top of the screen and slide your finger down. The Notifications appear.

2. Touch the ⚙ icon in the upper right-hand corner of the screen. The Settings screen appears.

3. Touch the 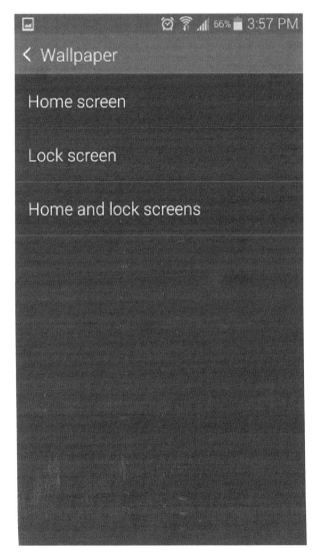 icon at the top of the screen. The Wallpaper Settings screen appears, as shown in **Figure 4**.

4. Touch **Home screen**, **Lock screen**, or **Home and lock screens** to set the wallpaper for the corresponding screen(s). The Wallpaper Selection menu appears, as shown in **Figure 5**.

5. Touch a picture, and then touch **Set wallpaper** at the top of the screen. The wallpaper is set. You may also touch **More images** to select an image from your Gallery.

Note: When using an image from the Gallery, you may need to crop it. Refer to "Editing a Photo" *on page 128 to learn how.*

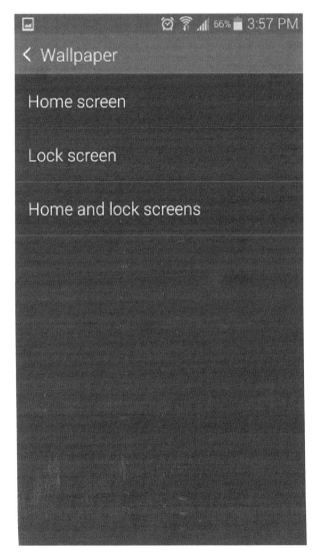

Figure 4: Wallpaper Settings Screen

Figure 5: Wallpaper Selection Menu

3. Turning Multi Window On or Off

The Galaxy S5 can split the screen in two and display two applications at once - a feature that is known as Multi Window. To use the Multi Window feature when it is activated, press and hold the 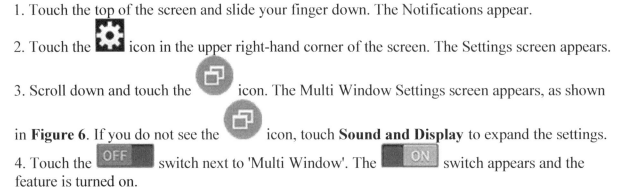 key. To activate Multi Window on or off:

1. Touch the top of the screen and slide your finger down. The Notifications appear.

2. Touch the ⚙ icon in the upper right-hand corner of the screen. The Settings screen appears.

3. Scroll down and touch the ⬛ icon. The Multi Window Settings screen appears, as shown in **Figure 6**. If you do not see the ⬛ icon, touch **Sound and Display** to expand the settings.

4. Touch the OFF switch next to 'Multi Window'. The ON switch appears and the feature is turned on.

5. Touch the ON switch next to 'Multi Window'. The OFF switch appears and the feature is turned off.

Note: Refer to "Tips and Tricks" on page 305 to learn how to use the Multi Window feature.

Figure 6: Multi Window Settings Screen

4. Turning Auto-Rotate On or Off

In most applications, the screen will automatically rotate when the phone is rotated. By default, Auto-Rotate is turned on. To turn Auto-Rotate on or off:

1. Touch the top of the screen and slide your finger down. The Notifications appear.

2. Touch the icon in the upper right-hand corner of the screen. The Settings screen appears.

3. Touch the [icon] icon at the top of the screen. The Display Settings screen appears.

4. Touch **Screen rotation**. The Screen Orientation Settings screen appears, as shown in **Figure 7**.

5. Touch the [ON] switch next to 'Screen Rotation'. The [OFF] switch appears and the screen will no longer rotate automatically.

6. Touch the [OFF] switch next to 'Screen Rotation'. The [ON] switch appears and the screen will rotate automatically.

7. You can also touch **Smart rotation** to make the phone rotate with your face, which is especially useful in preventing the screen from rotating when lying on your side in bed.

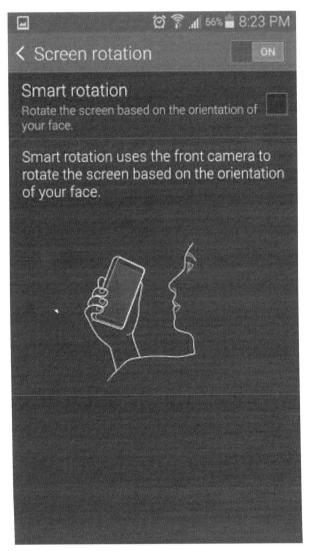

Figure 7: Screen Orientation Settings Screen

5. Setting the Screen Timeout

The screen timeout can be adjusted to automatically lock the Galaxy S5 after it is idle for a set period of time. To change the screen timeout:

1. Touch the top of the screen and slide your finger down. The Notifications appear.
2. Touch the ⚙ icon in the upper right-hand corner of the screen. The Settings screen appears.
3. Touch the icon at the top of the screen. The Display Settings screen appears.
4. Touch **Screen timeout**. The Screen Timeout settings appear, as shown in **Figure 8**.
5. Touch an option in the menu, indicating how long the phone will be idle before it locks itself. The screen timeout is set.

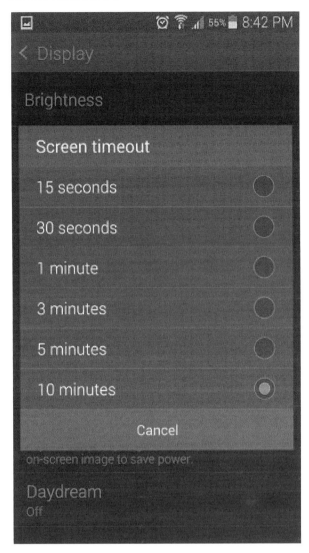

Figure 8: Screen Timeout Settings

6. Changing the Font

The Galaxy S5 allows you to customize the type of font that is used in menus, certain applications, and when entering text. You can also adjust the size of the font. To change the font:

1. Touch the top of the screen and slide your finger down. The Notifications appear.

2. Touch the ⚙ icon in the upper right-hand corner of the screen. The Settings screen appears.

3. Touch the  icon at the top of the screen. The Display Settings screen appears.
4. Touch **Font**. The Font menu appears, as shown in **Figure 9**.
5. Touch **Font Style**. A list of available fonts appears, as shown in **Figure 10**.
6. Touch a font in the list. A confirmation dialog appears.
7. Touch **Yes**. The new font style is applied.
8. Touch **Font size**. The Font Size menu appears, as shown in **Figure 11**.
9. Touch a font size in the list. The new font size is applied.

Figure 9: Font Menu

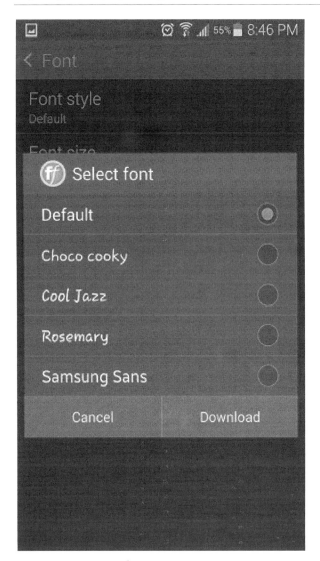

Figure 10: Font Style Menu

Figure 11: Font Size Menu

7. Setting the Touch Key Light Duration

The ⬜ and ↩ soft keys, also known as the touch keys, light up only when they are needed or when they are touched. The amount of time that they stay lit while not being touched can be customized. To set the soft key light duration:

1. Touch the top of the screen and slide your finger down. The Notifications appear.

2. Touch the 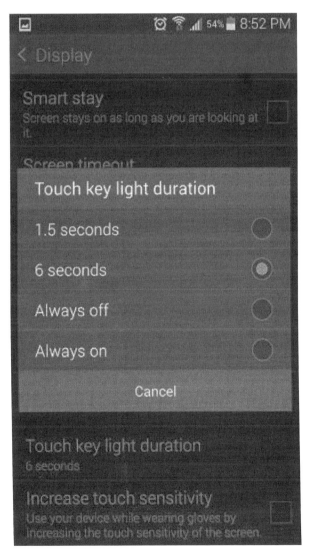 icon in the upper right-hand corner of the screen. The Settings screen appears.

3. Touch the icon at the top of the screen. The Display Settings screen appears.
4. Scroll down and touch **Touch key light duration**. The Touch Key Light Duration menu appears, as shown in **Figure 12**.
5. Touch one of the options in the menu. Selecting **Always off** will keep the soft key light off at all times. Selecting **Always on** will keep the soft key light on at all times. The soft key light duration is set.

Figure 12: Touch Key Light Duration Menu

8. Turning the Battery Percentage On or Off

The Galaxy S5 can display the exact percentage of battery life remaining in the upper right-hand corner of the screen. By default, this feature is turned on. To turn the battery percentage on or off:

1. Touch the top of the screen and slide your finger down. The Notifications appear.

2. Touch the ⚙ icon in the upper right-hand corner of the screen. The Settings screen appears.

3. Touch the 🔋 icon. The Battery screen appears, as shown in **Figure 13**. If you do not see the 🔋 icon, touch **System** to expand the settings.

4. Touch **Show battery percentage**. The ✔ mark next to 'Show battery percentage' disappears, and the battery percentage is hidden.

5. Touch **Show battery percentage** again. The ✔ mark reappears, and the battery percentage is shown in the upper right-hand corner of the screen, as outlined in red in **Figure 14**.

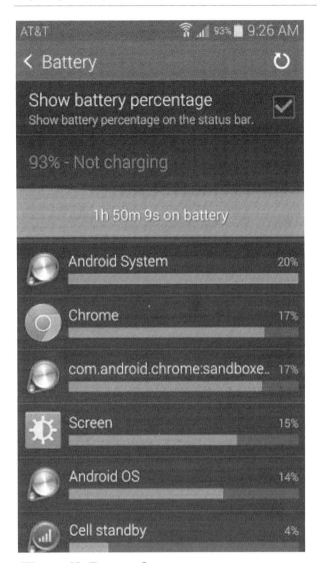

Figure 13: Battery Screen

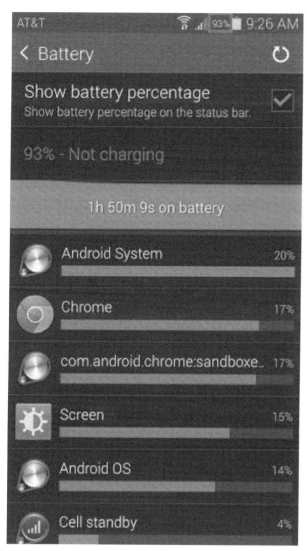

Figure 14: Battery Percentage

9. Turning High Touch Sensitivity On or Off

The touchscreen on most smartphones only responds when you touch it using bare skin. The touchscreen on the Galaxy S5 can be set to respond when you touch it while wearing gloves. To turn high touch sensitivity on or off:

1. Touch the top of the screen and slide your finger down. The Notifications appear.

2. Touch the ⚙ icon in the upper right-hand corner of the screen. The Settings screen appears.

3. Touch the ▫ icon at the top of the screen. The Display Settings screen appears.

4. Scroll down and touch **Increase touch sensitivity**. A ✓ mark appears and touch sensitivity is increased.

5. Touch **Increase touch sensitivity** again. The ✓ mark disappears and the feature is turned off.

10. Setting the Home Screen Mode

Depending on the amount of experience you have with Android phones, you may wish to use a simpler Home screen in order to avoid being overwhelmed. To set the Home Screen mode:

1. Touch the top of the screen and slide your finger down. The Notifications appear.

2. Touch the ⚙ icon in the upper right-hand corner of the screen. The Settings screen appears.

3. Touch the ⌂ icon. The Mode Settings screen appears, as shown in **Figure 15**.

4. Touch **Easy mode** if you are new to Android phones. Easy Mode is selected.

5. Touch **Done** at the top of the screen. The selected mode is applied.

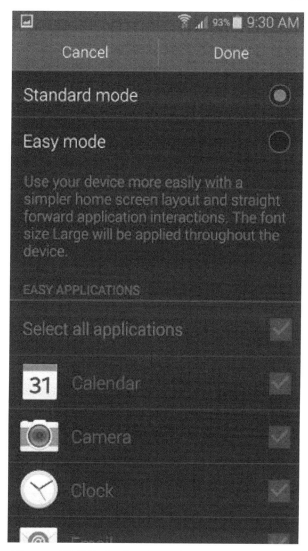

Figure 15: Mode Settings Screen

11. Turning Motions and Gestures On or Off

The Galaxy S5 allows you to perform certain tasks without touching the screen by using its sensor, which is located near the earpiece. To turn motions and gestures on or off:

1. Touch the top of the screen and slide your finger down. The Notifications appear.

2. Touch the ⚙ icon in the upper right-hand corner of the screen. The Settings screen appears.

3. Touch the ![icon] icon. The Motions and Gestures screen appears, as shown in **Figure 16**.
4. Touch one of the following options to turn the corresponding motions or gestures on or off:

Air browse

Touch the ![OFF] switch at the top of the screen after touching 'Air browse' to turn on the feature. Then, touch the ☐ next to one of the following options to turn it on, or touch the ✓ to turn it off:

- **The body of emails** - Allows you to wave your hand above the top of the phone to scroll through an email.
- **Gallery** - Allows you to scroll through pictures in the gallery by moving your hand from left to right or right to left.
- **Internet** - Allows you to scroll through a web page and switch between open tabs in the Internet browser (only works in the phone's Internet app).
- **Music** - Allows you to skip to the next track, rewind the current track, or return to the previous track by waving your hand to the left or right above the phone while using the Music application (only works in the phone's Internet app).
- **Music on lock screen** - Allows you to skip to the next track, rewind the current track, or return to the previous track by waving your hand to the left or right above the phone while music is playing and the screen is locked (only works with).

Direct call

Allows you to call the contact whose information is currently on the screen by putting the phone up to your ear. Touch the ![OFF] switch at the top of the screen after touching 'Direct call' to turn on the feature.

Smart alert

Causes the phone to briefly vibrate when it is picked up if there is a missed call or a new text message. Touch the ![OFF] switch at the top of the screen after touching 'Smart alert' to turn on the feature.

Mute/pause

Allows you to mute incoming calls and pause music by turning the phone over and laying it on its screen while the screen is turned on, or by covering the screen with your hand. Touch the ![OFF] switch at the top of the screen after touching 'Smart alert' to turn on the feature.

You may also touch Smart pause to turn on a feature that allows videos to be paused when you look away from the screen. 'Smart pause' only works in the Samsung Videos application.

Palm swipe to capture

Allows you to capture a screenshot by waving the side of your hand from left to right or right to left across the screen. Touch the OFF switch at the top of the screen after touching 'Palm swipe to capture' to turn on the feature.

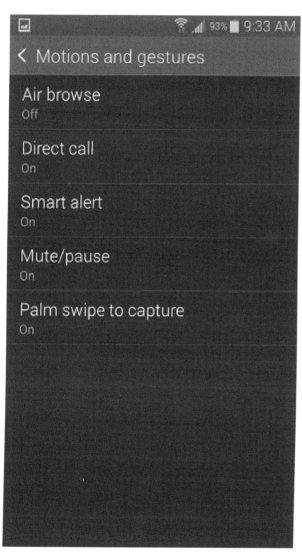

Figure 16: Motions and Gestures Screen

12. Turning Air View On or Off

The Air View features allow you to hover your finger over items on the screen in order to zoom in, or to view additional information. To turn Air View features on or off:

1. Touch the top of the screen and slide your finger down. The Notifications appear.

2. Touch the ⚙ icon in the upper right-hand corner of the screen. The Settings screen appears.

3. Scroll down and touch the 🔘 icon. The Air View settings appear, as shown in **Figure 17**.

4. Touch the **OFF** switch at the top of the screen. The **ON** switch appears, and Air View is turned on.

5. The following features are enabled when Air View is turned on:

   - **Calendar preview** - Allows you to preview calendar events for a specific day by hovering your finger over the day on the calendar.
   - **Gallery preview** - Allows you to preview the pictures in an album by hovering your finger over that album in the Gallery.
   - **Video preview** - Allows you to preview a scene in a video, or to view the elapsed time by hovering your finger over the progress bar.
   - **Phone magnifier** - Allows you to preview the contact assigned to a particular speed dial number by hovering your finger over that number.

Figure 17: Air View Settings

13. Customizing the LED Notification Light

The LED light to the right of the earpiece is used to notify you of certain events. To customize the LED notification light:

1. Touch the top of the screen and slide your finger down. The Notifications appear.

2. Touch the ⚙ icon in the upper right-hand corner of the screen. The Settings screen appears.

3. Touch the ⬜ icon at the top of the screen. The Display Settings screen appears.

4. Scroll down and touch **LED indicator**. The LED Indicator settings appear, as shown in **Figure 18**.

5. Touch one of the following options to turn it on or off:

   - **Charging** - Causes the red LED indicator to light up when the phone is charging and the screen is off.
   - **Low battery** - Causes the red LED to light up when the battery level is low and the screen is off.
   - **Notifications** - Causes the blue LED to light up when you have missed calls or messages and the screen is off.
   - **Voice recording** - Causes the blue LED to light up when you are recording voice with the screen turned off.

Figure 18: LED Indicator Settings

Adjusting the Security Settings

Table of Contents

1. Setting Up Screen Lock Protection
2. Changing the Automatic Lock Time
3. Making Passwords Visible
4. Allowing the Installation of Applications from Unknown Sources

1. Setting Up Screen Lock Protection

Setting a security lock can help to prevent unauthorized users from accessing your phone. There are five options for locking the screen: Swipe, Pattern, Personal Identification Number (PIN), Password, and Fingerprint. To set up Screen Lock Protection:

1. Touch the top of the screen and slide your finger down. The Notifications appear, as shown in **Figure 1**.

2. Touch the ⚙ icon in the upper right-hand corner of the screen. The Settings screen appears, as shown in **Figure 2**.

3. Scroll down and touch the 🔒 icon at the top of the screen. The Lock Screen menu appears, as shown in **Figure 3**.

4. Touch **Screen lock**. The Screen Lock Selection menu appears, as shown in **Figure 4**.

5. Touch one of the following options to set the corresponding Screen Lock:

   - **Swipe** - Touch anywhere on the lock screen and swipe in any direction to unlock the phone. No setup is required for this method. This method does not provide any security.
   - **Pattern** - Draw a pattern on the screen. This method provides medium security.
   - **Fingerprint** - Swipe your finger to unlock the screen. The fingerprint scanner will only respond to the registered fingerprints. You may register up to three fingerprints. This method provides medium high security.
   - **PIN**- Enter a series of numbers to use as a passcode. This method provides medium high security.
   - **Password** - Enter an alphanumeric code. This method provides the highest level of security.

- **None** - The screen will turn off, but the phone will not lock. No setup is required for this method.

To set up a pattern lock:

- Touch **Pattern**. The Pattern screen appears.
- Draw the desired pattern. The pattern is entered.
- Touch **Continue**. A confirmation screen appears.
- Draw the same pattern again. The pattern is stored.
- Touch **Confirm**. The Pattern lock is set, and the backup PIN screen appears. You will need to enter the PIN twice.
- When you are done, touch **OK**. The pattern lock is set.

To set up a fingerprint lock:

1. Touch **Fingerprint**. The Fingerprint Registration screen appears.

2. Swipe the pad on the screen, as shown in the animation. You will need to swipe the pad eight times. The password screen appears.
3. Enter a backup password in case using your fingerprint does not work. Touch **OK** when you are finished.

Note: If you are having trouble unlocking the phone using your fingerprint, try using the same finger that you used when you registered your fingerprint.

To set up a PIN lock:

- Touch **PIN**. The PIN Lock screen appears.
- Enter the desired PIN. The PIN is entered. A PIN must be between four and 16 digits in length.
- Touch **Continue**. A confirmation screen appears.
- Enter the same PIN again. The PIN is entered.
- Touch **OK**. The PIN lock is set.

To set up a password lock:

1. Touch **Password**. The Password screen appears.
2. Enter the desired password. The password is entered. A password must be between four and 16 characters in length.
3. Touch **Continue**. A confirmation screen appears.
4. Enter the same password again. The password is entered.
5. Touch **OK**. The Password lock is set.

Note: Repeat this process to change the screen lock. You will need to enter the current screen lock to change it.

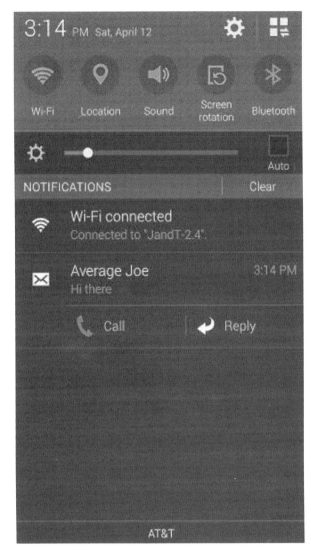

Figure 1: Notifications

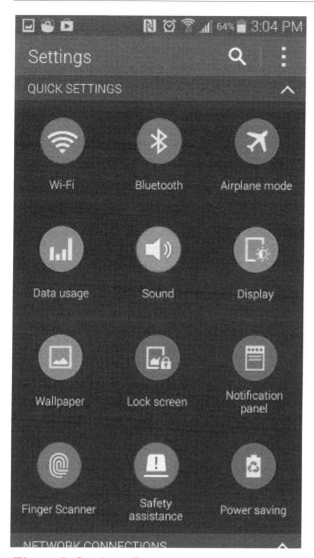

Figure 2: Settings Screen

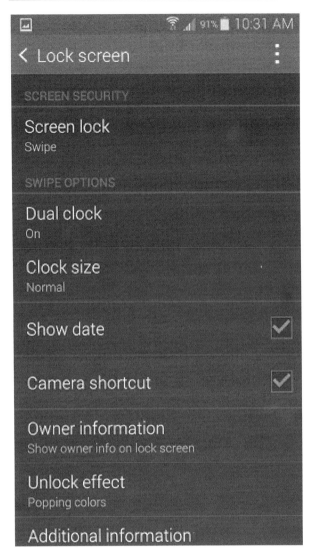

Figure 3: Lock Screen Menu

Figure 4: Screen Lock Selection Menu

2. Changing the Automatic Lock Time

After the Galaxy S5 is locked using the Power button, it will not require a password, pattern, or face to unlock it right away unless the lock time is set to 'Immediately'. The phone may be set to wait a certain amount of time before prompting for the screen lock. To change the Lock time:

Warning: Setting the Lock time to anything but 'Immediately' will leave your phone unprotected for the set period of time.

1. Touch the top of the screen and slide your finger down. The Notifications appear.

2. Touch the ⚙ icon in the upper right-hand corner of the screen. The Settings screen appears.

3. Scroll down and touch the 🔒 icon at the top of the screen. The Lock Screen menu appears.

4. Scroll down and touch **Secured lock time**. A list of lock time options appears, as shown in **Figure 5**.

5. Touch an option in the menu. The lock time is set. The phone will wait the selected interval before requesting a screen lock.

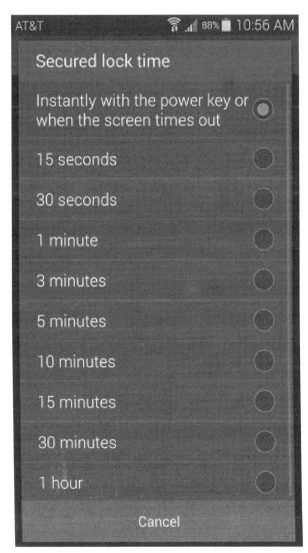

Figure 5: List of Lock Time Options

3. Making Passwords Visible

When entering a password, it can be concealed to prevent someone from viewing it over your shoulder. However, it may be more convenient to see what is being typed. To make passwords visible:

1. Touch the top of the screen and slide your finger down. The Notifications appear.

2. Touch the [icon] icon in the upper right-hand corner of the screen. The Settings screen appears.

3. Scroll down and touch the [icon] icon at the top of the screen. The Security Settings appear, as shown in **Figure 6**. If you do not see the [icon] icon, touch **System** to expand the settings.

4. Touch **Make passwords visible**. A ✓ mark appears next to 'Make passwords visible', and the feature is turned on.

5. Touch **Make passwords visible** again. The ✓ mark disappears, and the feature is turned off.

Figure 6: Security Settings

4. Allowing the Installation of Applications from Unknown Sources

If you wish to install applications from sources other than the Play Store, you must first set the Galaxy S5 to allow such installations. To allow the installation of applications from unknown sources:

1. Touch the top of the screen and slide your finger down. The Notifications appear.

2. Touch the [icon] icon in the upper right-hand corner of the screen. The Settings screen appears.

3. Scroll down and touch the [icon] icon at the top of the screen. The Security Settings appear. If you do not see the [icon] icon, touch **System** to expand the settings.

4. Scroll down and touch **Unknown sources**. A confirmation dialog appears.

5. Touch **OK**. A [check mark] mark appears next to 'Unknown sources', and the feature is turned on.

6. Touch **Unknown sources** again. The [check mark] mark disappears, and the feature is turned off.

Adjusting the Language and Input Settings

Table of Contents

1. Changing the Phone Language
2. Adding an Input Language
3. Personalizing Text Prediction
4. Turning SwiftKey Flow On or Off

1. Changing the Phone Language

The Galaxy S5 has six built-in languages from which to choose. Setting an alternative phone language will make all menu options and buttons appear in the selected language. Web pages and other content will still be displayed in the language in which they were originally written. To change the phone language:

1. Touch the top of the screen and slide your finger down. The Notifications appear, as shown in **Figure 1**.

2. Touch the icon in the upper right-hand corner of the screen. The Settings screen appears, as shown in **Figure 2**.

3. Scroll down and touch the icon at the top of the screen. The Language and Input Settings appear, as shown in **Figure 3**. If you do not see the icon, scroll down and touch **System** to expand the settings.

4. Touch **Language**. A list of available languages appears, as shown in **Figure 4**.

5. Touch a language. The phone's language is changed to the selected option.

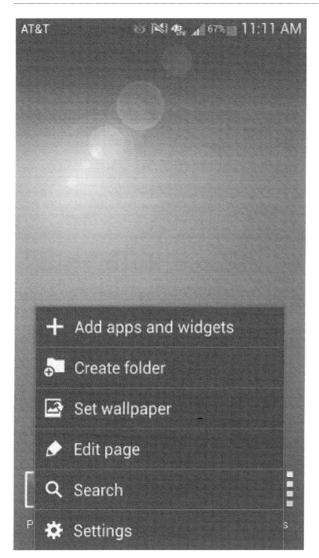

Figure 1: Home Screen Menu

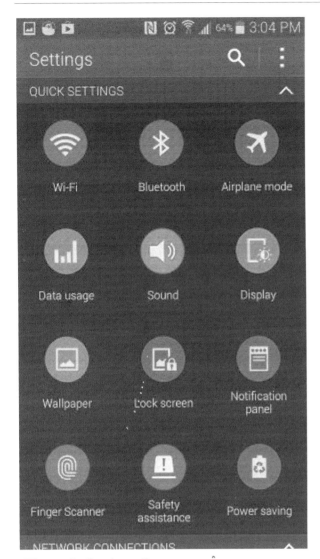

Figure 2: Settings Screen

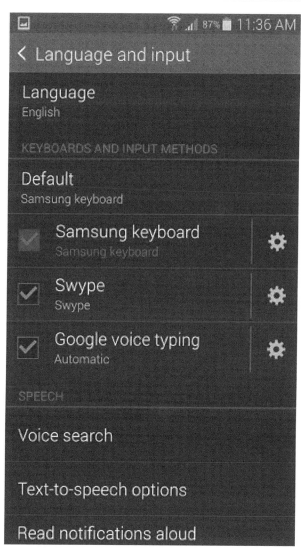

Figure 3: Language and Input Settings Screen

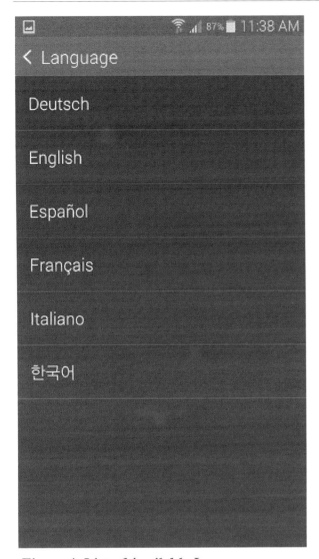

Figure 4: List of Available Languages

2. Adding an Input Language

The Galaxy S5 allows you to enter text in many different languages by using alternative keyboards. To switch to an alternative keyboard at any time, touch the space bar and slide your finger to the left or right. To add an input language:

1. Touch the top of the screen and slide your finger down. The Notifications appear.
2. Touch the ⚙ icon in the upper right-hand corner of the screen. The Settings screen appears.
3. Scroll down and touch the Ⓐ icon at the top of the screen. The Language and Input Settings appear. If you do not see the Ⓐ icon, scroll down and touch **System** to expand the settings.
4. Touch the ⚙ icon next to 'Samsung Keyboard'. The Samsung Keyboard Settings appear, as shown in **Figure 5**.
5. Touch **Select input languages**. A list of available keyboards appears, as shown in **Figure 6**.
6. Touch a language. A ✓ mark appears next to the language, and the corresponding keyboard is now available when entering text. The phone may need to download the language, which will occur automatically. In this case, you will need to repeat this step, and touch the language under 'Downloaded languages' to add it.

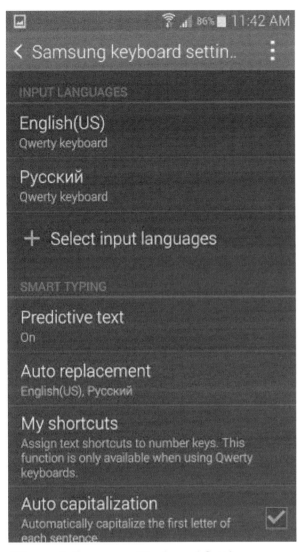

Figure 5: Samsung Keyboard Settings

Figure 6: List of Available Keyboards

3. Personalizing Text Prediction

While entering text, the Galaxy S5 can guess the word that you are trying to enter, and guess the next word that you may wish to type. You will then receive suggestions based on what you have already typed. This feature allows you to enter text more quickly. In addition, the keyboard can learn from your text messages, emails, and social networks, making predictions more accurate. To turn predictive text on or off:

1. Touch the top of the screen and slide your finger down. The Notifications appear.

2. Touch the ⚙ icon in the upper right-hand corner of the screen. The Settings screen appears.

3. Scroll down and touch the Ⓐ icon at the top of the screen. The Language and Input Settings appear. If you do not see the Ⓐ icon, scroll down and touch **System** to expand the settings.

4. Touch the ⚙ icon next to 'Samsung Keyboard'. The Samsung Keyboard Settings appear. By default, predictive text is turned on. You can always touch the ▬▬ ON switch next to 'Predictive text' to turn it off.

5. Touch **Predictive text**. The Predictive Text settings appear, as shown in **Figure 7**. By default, personalized data is turned on. You can always touch **Personalized data** to clear the ✓ mark and turn off the feature. This will not turn the predictive text feature off.

6. Touch one of the **Learn from** options in the menu. You may need to log in to your account in order to have the phone learn from your typing style. The keyboard is now customized based on your messages, emails, or social networks.

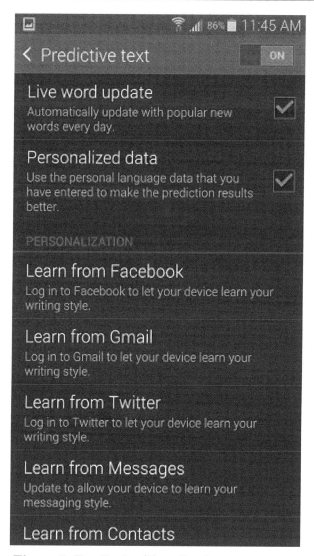

Figure 7: Predictive Text Settings

4. Turning Swype On or Off

The Swype feature allows you to enter text by touching the first letter of a word, and then sliding your finger to each subsequent letter without releasing the screen. After you have reached the final letter, release the screen to enter the word. To turn Swype on or off:

1. Touch the top of the screen and slide your finger down. The Notifications appear.

2. Touch the ⚙ icon in the upper right-hand corner of the screen. The Settings screen appears.

3. Scroll down and touch the Ⓐ icon at the top of the screen. The Language and Input Settings appear. If you do not see the Ⓐ icon, scroll down and touch **System** to expand the settings.

4. Touch **Swype**. The ✓ mark next to 'Swype' disappears, and the feature is turned off.

5. Touch **Swype** again. The ✓ mark appears, and the feature is turned on.

Tips and Tricks

Table of Contents

1. Maximizing Battery Life
2. Adding an Extension to a Contact's Number
3. Checking the Amount of Available Memory
4. Calling a Number from a Website
5. Locking Text Messages
6. Entering Alternative Characters
7. Using MP3's as Ringtones
8. Capturing a Screenshot without Connecting the Phone to a Computer
9. Viewing All Quick Settings Icons in the Notification Bar
10. Clearing a Single Notification
11. Blocking Calls, Notifications, Alarms, and the LED Indicator
12. Viewing a Video while Using Another Application
13. Making the Phone Open Applications and Menus Faster (Advanced Tip)\
14. Making the Home Button More Responsive
15. Hiding Personal Files

1. Maximizing Battery Life

There are several things you can do to increase the battery life of the Galaxy S5:

- Lock the phone whenever it is not in use. Because of its size and power, leaving the screen turned on will quickly kill the battery. To lock the phone, press the **Power** button once.
- Keep the Timeout Setting set to a small amount of time. This will dim and turn off the screen when the phone is idle. Refer to *"Setting the Screen Timeout"* on page 267 to learn how to adjust the Timeout setting.
- Turn down the brightness or turn on auto-brightness. To learn how to adjust the brightness, refer to *"Adjusting the Brightness"* on page 258.
- Turn off Bluetooth when not in use. Keep Wi-Fi turned on, since the mobile network, which is responsible for data, is not in use when Wi-Fi is turned on. The mobile network will keep searching for signal, especially in an area with low signal, which can decrease battery life. Refer to *"Setting Up Wi-Fi"* on page 233 to learn how to turn on Wi-Fi. Refer to *"Setting Up Bluetooth"* on page 237 to learn how to turn off Bluetooth.

- Avoid using the camera and do not use the camera flash, if possible. Both need a lot of battery power to operate.
- Activate Ultra Power Saving mode if your battery is low and you do not have access to a charger. To do so, touch the top of the screen and slide your finger down to access the Notifications. Then, touch **U. power saving**.

2. Adding an Extension to a Contact's Number

When entering a number for a stored contact, you may also add an extension that will be dialed following a two-second pause after the number is dialed. To add an extension, add Pauses (found by touching the [Sym] key on the keypad) after the number. Touch the [Pause(,)] key, and then add the extension following the pause. You may also touch the [Wait(;)] key to make the phone wait until it is safe to enter an extension. Whether you should use a Pause or touch **WAIT** depends on the number that you dial.

3. Checking the Amount of Available Memory

To check the amount of available memory at any time, touch the [icon] key. A list of open applications appears. Touch the [icon] icon at the bottom of the screen. The amount of available memory on the device and the SD card is shown under 'RAM Status'. You can also view the amount of available memory on the phone and SD card by touching the [icon] icon from the Settings screen.

4. Calling a Number from a Website

A phone number can be dialed directly from a website. Most phone numbers that can be dialed are displayed in a blue box, although this also works for those that do not formally appear in blue.

Touch the phone number. The keypad appears and the number is entered. Touch the [icon] button at the bottom of the screen. The phone dials the number.

5. Locking Text Messages

Text messages can be locked to prevent accidental deletion. When deleting an entire conversation, all of the unlocked text messages are deleted, unless "Delete locked messages" is checked. By default, "Delete locked messages" is unchecked. Refer to *"Deleting Text Messages"* on page 79 to learn more. To lock a message:

1. Touch the [icon] icon. The Messaging screen appears.
2. Touch a conversation. The Conversation opens.
3. Touch and hold a text message. The Message options appear
4. Touch **Lock**. The text message is locked. To unlock the text message, follow steps 1-3 and then touch **Unlock**.

6. Entering Alternative Characters

While typing a sentence, insert other letters, such as Á or Ñ, by touching and holding the base letter. A menu of characters appears above the letter. Slide your finger to a character to insert it. The highlighted letter is inserted.

7. Using MP3's as Ringtones

You can set any song in your personal music library as your phone's ringtone or a custom ringtone for a contact. To use an MP3 as a ringtone:

1. Touch the [icon] icon at the bottom of the Home screen. The Application screen appears.
2. Touch the [icon] icon. The Music application opens.
3. Find the song that you wish to set as a ringtone. You can browse music by touching one of the icons at the top of the screen, such as Artists.
4. Touch and hold the song. The Song is selected.
5. Touch the [icon] icon. The Song menu appears.
6. Touch **Set as**. The Ringtone menu appears.
7. Touch **From the beginning** to use the entire song, or touch **Auto recommendations** to use only part of the song, as recommended by other people.

8. Touch **Phone ringtone** to set the song as the default ringtone or touch **Caller ringtone** to set the song as a custom ringtone for the selected contact.
9. Touch **OK** in the upper right-hand corner of the screen. The song is set as the ringtone.

8. Capturing a Screenshot without Connecting the Phone to a Computer

To capture a screenshot, press the **Power** button and **Home** button at exactly the same time. Hold the buttons for two seconds. A framed picture of the current screen briefly appears and a screenshot is captured. Release the buttons. The screenshot can be found in the 'Screenshots' album in the Gallery.

9. Viewing All Quick Settings Icons in the Notification Bar

You do not have to go through the Application screen to adjust certain Phone settings. Touch the Notification bar at the top of the screen using two fingers and slide down. A list of all quick settings icons appears.

10. Clearing a Single Notification

While viewing notifications on the Notification screen (opened by touching the status bar and sliding your finger down), you can clear one notification at a time. Touch the notification and slide your finger to the left or right. The notification is cleared.

11. Blocking Calls, Notifications, Alarms, and the LED Indicator

If you do not wish to be disturbed during a certain time, you may turn on Blocking Mode to prevent the phone from receiving calls, or notifying you of events. To turn on Blocking Mode:

1. Touch the top of the screen and slide your finger down. The Notifications appear.

2. Touch the ⚙ icon in the upper right-hand corner of the screen. The Settings screen appears.

3. Scroll down and touch the 🔘 icon. The Blocking Mode screen appears.

4. Touch the `OFF` switch next to Blocking mode. Blocking mode is turned on, and additional options become available.

5. Touch one of the options under 'Features' to customize the features that should be blocked.

6. Touch **Always** under 'Set time' to permanently turn on Blocking mode. You can always turn it off by touching the `ON` switch next to 'Blocking mode'.

7. Touch **Always** to clear the ✓ mark and set the times during which Blocking mode should automatically turn on. You can do this by touching the times next to 'From' and 'To'.

8. Touch **Allowed contacts** to customize the list of contacts that you wish to allow.

12. Viewing a Video while Using Another Application

The video player on the Galaxy S5 allows you to view a video in a movable window while viewing the Home screen or in another application. Only certain applications, such as Samsung's Internet application, are able to take advantage of this feature. To view a video while using another application, touch Video player when the phone asks you how you would like to play a video.

Then, touch the 🔲 icon. The video pops out and is displayed in a window. You can also move the window around by dragging it with your finger, or pause it by touching it once. When the video ends, the window automatically disappears.

13. Making the Phone Open Applications and Menus Faster (Advanced Tip)

You may notice that the Galaxy S5 can become a bit choppy when unlocking or switching from one screen to another. This effect is present because of the phone's animated transitions, which can be turned off under the developer settings. To turn off transition animations and speed up the phone:

Warning: This tip is for advanced users ONLY. Any attempt to edit any other developer settings other than the ones mentioned in the steps below may bring harm to your phone.

1. Touch the top of the screen and slide your finger down. The Notifications appear.

2. Touch the ⚙ icon in the upper right-hand corner of the screen. The Settings screen appears.

3. Scroll down and touch the ⓘ icon. The About Device screen appears.
4. Scroll down and touch **Build number** seven times. Developer options are now enabled.

5. Touch the ⬑ key, and then touch the {} icon. The Developer options appear.
6. Make sure all three of the following options are set to off:

- **Window animation scale**
- **Transition animation scale**
- **Animator duration scale**

Your phone will no longer lag when unlocking and opening applications.

14. Making the Home Button More Responsive

The Home button can be a little slow because when you press it once, the phone waits to see whether you are going to press it again to activate the S Voice assistant. To speed up the Home button, disable the S Voice shortcut by doing the following:

1. Touch the top of the screen and slide your finger down. The Notifications appear.

2. Touch the ⚙ icon in the upper right-hand corner of the screen. The Settings screen appears.

3. Scroll down and touch the 🎤 icon. The S Voice Settings screen appears.
4. Touch **Open via the home key**. The ✓ disappears and the Home button will now be more responsive.

15. Hiding Personal Files

If you store files on the phone that you do not wish anyone else to see, especially if you lose the phone, you may activate Private mode to hide those files. To activate Private mode:

1. Touch the top of the screen and slide your finger down. The Notifications appear.
2. Touch the ⚙ icon in the upper right-hand corner of the screen. The Settings screen appears.
3. Scroll down and touch the 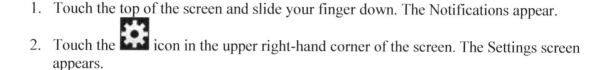 icon. The Private Mode Settings screen appears.
4. Touch the OFF switch next to 'Private mode'. Private mode is turned on. You will need to set up an unlock method, such as a PIN or password.
5. Touch and hold any content that you wish to hide, such as photos, and then touch **Hide** in the content menu. You will need to touch the ⋮ icon to access the content menus.
6. Touch the ON switch next to 'Private mode' to turn it off and hide the content that you selected.

Troubleshooting

Table of Contents

1. Galaxy S5 does not turn on
2. Galaxy S5 is not responding
3. Can't make a call
4. Can't surf the web
5. Screen or keyboard does not rotate
6. Low Microphone Volume, Caller can't hear you
7. Display does not adjust brightness automatically
8. Application does not install correctly
9. Touchscreen does not respond as expected
10. Phone becomes very hot
11. Camera does not turn on

1. Galaxy S5 does not turn on

If the Galaxy S5 does not turn on:

- **Recharge the phone** - Use the included wall charger to charge the battery. If the battery power is extremely low, the screen will not turn on for several minutes. Do NOT attempt to use the USB port on your computer to charge the phone, as it will not work.
- **Replace the battery** - If you purchased the phone a long time ago, you may need to replace the battery. In this case, however, the phone may still turn on, but the battery will die much faster than it would in a newer one.
- **Perform a Soft Reset** - If you have done one or both of the above and the phone still does not start, a soft reset should be performed. To perform a soft reset:

  1. Press and hold the **Power** button, and then touch **Power off**. The phone turns off.
  2. Take out the battery and wait ten seconds. The phone resets.
  3. Re-insert the battery. Press and hold the **Power** button for three seconds. The phone turns on.

2. Galaxy S5 is not responding

If the phone is frozen or is not responding, try one or more of the following. These steps typically solve most problems on the phone:

- **Restart the phone** - If the phone freezes while running an application, try holding down the **Power** button. If this does not work, the best course of action is to perform a soft reset. Refer to *"Perform a Soft Reset"* on page 312 to learn how.
- **Remove Media** - Some downloaded applications or music may freeze up the phone. After restarting the phone, try deleting some of the media. To learn how to delete an application, refer to *"Uninstalling an Application"* on page 216. You may also erase all data at once and reset your phone to factory defaults by doing the following:

Warning: Any erased data is not recoverable.

1. Touch the top of the screen and slide your finger down. The Notifications appear.
2. Touch the ⚙ icon in the upper right-hand corner of the screen. The Settings screen appears.
3. Scroll down and touch the 🗄 icon at the top of the screen. The Backup and Reset screen appears.
4. Touch **Factory Data Reset**. The Reset screen appears.
5. Touch **Reset device**. A confirmation dialog appears.
6. Touch **Delete all**. All data is erased and the phone resets.

3. Can't make a call

If you cannot make a call using the phone, check the following:

- **Service** - If there are no bars shown at the top right of the screen, then the network does not cover you in your location. Try walking to a different location or even to a different part of a building.
- **Airplane Mode** - Make sure Airplane mode is turned off. If it is already off, try turning Airplane mode on for 15 seconds and then turning it back off. Refer to *"Turning Airplane Mode On or Off"* on page 239 to learn how to turn Airplane mode off.
- **Area code** - Make sure you dialed an area code with the phone number.
- **Restart** - Turn the phone off and back on, as this sometimes solves the problem.

4. Can't surf the web

Make sure the mobile network or Wi-Fi is turned on. Refer to *"Enabling or Disabling the Mobile Network"* on page 241 or refer to *"Setting Up Wi-Fi"* on page 233 to learn more.

5. Screen or keyboard does not rotate

If the screen does not turn or the full, horizontal keyboard is not showing when the phone is turned on its side, the problem may be one of the following issues:

- It is very likely that the application does not support the horizontal view.
- Make sure that the phone is not lying flat while rotating. Hold the phone upright to change the orientation in applications that support it.
- Make sure auto-rotate is turned on. Refer to *"Turning Auto-Rotate On and Off"* on page 265 to learn more.

6. Low microphone volume, caller can't hear you

If you are talking to someone who can't hear you, try removing any cases or other accessories, as these may cover up the microphone. If the caller cannot hear you at all, you may have accidentally muted the conversation. To learn how to turn mute on or off while on a call, refer to *"Using the Mute Function During a Voice Call"* on page 42.

If you find yourself accidentally muting the conversation too often, there may be something covering up the light sensor, preventing the screen from dimming and locking the mute button. Taking off any accessories may also correct this problem, as some low-end cases may cover up the sensor completely.

7. Display does not adjust brightness automatically

If the phone does not dim in dark conditions or does not become brighter in bright conditions, try taking any cases or accessories off. Cases may block the light sensor at the top of the phone, located near the earpiece. Also, Auto Brightness may be turned off. To learn how to turn Auto Brightness on or off, refer to *"Adjusting the Brightness"* on page 258.

8. Application does not install correctly

Sometimes applications may not download or install correctly. If this happens, try canceling the download and re-downloading the application. If the application is already installed, try uninstalling and re-installing it. Refer to *"Uninstalling an Application"* on page 216 to learn more.

9. Touchscreen does not respond as expected

If there is a problem with the touchscreen, try the following, in the order in which the steps appear:

1. Remove any cases or screen protectors from the touchscreen.
2. Clean the screen with a soft, damp cloth.
3. Wash and dry your hands thoroughly. Grease and other residue on your skin may cause the touchscreen to function improperly.
4. Restart your device to clear any temporary software bugs.

10. Phone becomes very hot

Some applications require a lot of power and may cause the phone to become hot to the touch. This is normal and should not affect your device's life span or performance.

11. Camera does not turn on

If the camera does not turn on, try one of the following:

- Free up some memory by transferring files to a PC or deleting files from your device, as there may not be enough remaining memory to store new pictures. The camera may not turn on if the memory is too low.
- Restart the phone and try turning on the camera again.

Index

A

Adding a Contact Shortcut to the Home Screen, 65
Adding a Contact to a Group, 61
Adding a Contact to Favorites, 63
Adding a Contact to the Reject List, 63
Adding a Google Account to the Phone, 184
Adding a New Contact, 45
Adding an Application to Your Wishlist, 218
Adding an Attachment to a Text Message, 84
Adding an Email Account to the Phone, 171
Adding an Extension to a Contact's Number, 306
Adding an Input Language, 299
Adding and Viewing Bookmarks, 148
Adding Labels to Emails, 198
Adding Texted Phone Numbers to Contacts, 80
Adjusting Gmail Account Preferences, 206
Adjusting the Brightness, 258
Adjusting the Display Settings, 258
Adjusting the General Gmail Preferences, 202
Adjusting the Language and Input Settings, 294
Adjusting the Security Settings, 284
Adjusting the Sound Settings, 246
Adjusting the Wireless Settings, 233
Allowing the Installation of Applications from Unknown Sources, 293
Application does not install correctly, 315
Applying an Effect before Taking a Picture, 111
Asking about the Weather, 232
Assigning a Photo to a Contact, 52
Attaching a Calendar Event, 95
Attaching a Memo, 93
Attaching a Picture, 86
Attaching a Video, 90
Attaching a Voice Recording, 91

B

Backing Up Contacts, 61
Blocking All Emails from a Specific Sender, 182, 201
Blocking Calls, Notifications, Alarms, and the LED Indicator, 308
Browsing Photos and Videos, 122
Button Layout, 8
Buying an Application, 214

C

Calling a Contact, 30
Calling a Frequently Dialed Number, 32
Calling a Number from a Website, 306
Calling the Sender from within a Text, 77
Calling, Sending Messages, and Taking Notes, 229
Camera does not turn on, 315
Can't make a call, 313
Can't surf the web, 314
Capturing a Screenshot without Connecting the Phone to a Computer, 308
Capturing a Video, 117
Changing the Automatic Lock Time, 289
Changing the Font, 268
Changing the Phone Language, 294
Changing the Text Size, 166
Changing the Wallpaper, 261
Charging the Galaxy S5, 13
Checking the Amount of Available Memory, 306
Clearing a Single Notification, 308
Clearing Personal Data, 168
Closing Applications Running in the Background, 222
Composing a New Text Message, 67
Copying, Cutting, and Pasting Text, 70
Creating a Panoramic Photo, 116
Creating a Photo Collage, 144
Creating an Animated Photo, 114
Customizing the LED Notification Light, 282

D

Deleting a Contact, 50
Deleting Emails and Restoring Deleted Emails to the Inbox (Email App), 179
Deleting Emails and Restoring Deleted Emails to the Inbox (Gmail App), 194
Deleting Photos and Videos, 141
Deleting Text Messages, 79
Dialing a Number, 28
Display does not adjust brightness automatically, 314

E

Editing a Photo, 128
Editing Camera and Camcorder Settings, 120
Editing Contact Information, 48
Enabling or Disabling the Mobile Network, 241
Entering Alternative Characters, 307

F

Finding a Contact, 47
Finding Information about Music and Movies, 230
Finding Locations and Attractions, 231
Forwarding Text Messages, 76

G

Galaxy S5 does not turn on, 312
Galaxy S5 is not responding, 313
Getting Started, 8

H

Hiding Applications on the Application Screen, 220
Hiding Personal Files, 311

I

Ignoring New Messages in a Conversation, 201
Installing a Previously Purchased Application, 226

J

Joining or Separating Contact Information of Two Contacts, 65

L

Locking Text Messages, 307
Looking Up Times and Dates, 231
Low microphone volume, caller can't hear you, 314

M

Making Calls, 28
Making Passwords Visible, 291
Making the Home Button More Responsive, 310
Making the Phone Open Applications and Menus Faster (Advanced Tip), 309
Managing Applications, 208

Managing Browser Tabs, 151
Managing Contacts, 45
Managing Favorite Text Message Recipients, 101
Managing Photo and Video Albums, 122
Maximizing Battery Life, 305
Moving Photos between Albums, 142

N

Navigating the Screens, 15
Navigating to a Web Page, 147
Navigating to a Webpage, 230

O

Organizing Application Icons into Folders, 223
Organizing Home Screen Objects, 17

P

Personalizing Text Prediction, 302
Phone becomes very hot, 315

R

Reading Email (Email App), 174
Reading Email (Gmail App), 189
Reading Text Messages, 75
Receiving a Voice Call, 37
Receiving Text Messages, 73
Redialing the Last Dialed Number, 44
Replying to and Forwarding Emails (Email App), 177
Replying to and Forwarding Emails (Gmail App), 192
Returning a Recent Phone Call, 35

S

Saving Attachments from Text Messages, 97
Saving Passwords, 162
Screen or keyboard does not rotate, 314
Searching a Web Page for a Word or Phrase, 154
Searching for an Application, 209
Searching the Inbox (Email App), 181
Searching the Inbox (Gmail App), 200
Searching the Web for General Information, 230
Sending a Text Message to an Entire Group, 99
Sending an Email (Email App), 175
Sending an Email (Gmail App), 190
Setting the Camcorder Mode, 118
Setting the Camera Mode, 113
Setting the Default Notification Sound, 255
Setting the Default Ringtone, 252

Setting the Default Vibration Pattern, 253
Setting the Home Screen Mode, 276
Setting the Ringtone, Media, and Alarm Volume, 250
Setting the Screen Timeout, 267
Setting the Search Engine, 158
Setting the Touch Key Light Duration, 271
Setting the Vibration Intensity, 246
Setting Up a Google Account, 208
Setting Up Bluetooth, 237
Setting Up Screen Lock Protection, 284
Setting Up Wi-Fi, 233
Sharing a Contact's Information, 56
Sharing a Web Page, 157
Starting a Conference Call (Adding a Call), 44
Starting a Slideshow, 125
Switching between Google Accounts, 227
Switching to a Bluetooth Headset during a Voice Call, 42
Switching to another Language, 73

T

Tagging a Person in a Photo, 138
Taking a Picture, 105
Taking a Picture while Capturing a Video, 118
Taking Pictures and Capturing Videos, 105
Text Messaging, 67
Tips and Tricks, 305
Touchscreen does not respond as expected, 315
Transferring Files to the Galaxy S5 Using a PC or Mac / Inserting a microSD Card, 25
Trimming a Video, 140
Troubleshooting, 312
Turning Air View On or Off, 280
Turning Airplane Mode On or Off, 239
Turning Autofill On or Off, 160
Turning Auto-Rotate On or Off, 265
Turning Data Roaming On or Off, 243
Turning High Touch Sensitivity On or Off, 276
Turning Motions and Gestures On or Off, 277

Turning Multi Window On or Off, 264
Turning Near Field Communication On or Off, 244
Turning Pop-Up Blocking On or Off, 164
Turning Ringer Vibration On or Off, 256
Turning Swype On or Off, 304
Turning System Sounds On or Off, 257
Turning the Battery Percentage On or Off, 273
Turning the Galaxy S5 On and Off / Restarting the Phone, 14
Types of Home Screen Objects, 16

U

Uninstalling an Application, 216
Updating Installed Applications, 227
Using Both Cameras at Once, 107
Using MP3's as Ringtones, 307
Using the Auto-Complete Feature, 72
Using the Chrome Web Browser, 147
Using the Digital Zoom, 106
Using the Email Application, 171
Using the Flash, 110
Using the Gmail Application, 184
Using the Keypad during a Voice Call, 41
Using the Mute Function during a Voice Call, 42
Using the S Voice Assistant, 229
Using the Speakerphone during a Voice Call, 39

V

Viewing a Video while Using Another Application, 309
Viewing All Quick Settings Icons in the Notification Bar, 308
Viewing Sender Information from within a Text, 78
Viewing the Browsing History, 156

W

Working with Links, 153

Made in the USA
Lexington, KY
19 June 2014